Take Off Your Shoes:

Biblical Encounters with God

To Howard & Marilyn

Paul

Paul Hay

pastorpaulpoet.com

Table of Contents

Preface: Encounters With God..5

1. Where Are You? (Genesis 3:1-9)...8

2. Questions And Answers (Job 38-41)...................................14

3. Is Anything Too Hard For The Lord? (Genesis 18:1-15).......18

4. Your Only Son (Genesis 22:1-19).......................................23

5. Wrestling With God (Genesis 32:22-32).............................26

6. Who Am I? (Exodus 3:1-14)...31

7. Whose Side Are You On? (Joshua 5:13-15).........................35

8. I Will Hear From Heaven (2 Chronicles 7:1-22)..................38

9. A Still Small Voice (1 Kings 19:1-18)................................43

10. Here Am I (Isaiah 6:1-8)..48

11. I Am Only A Child (Jeremiah 1:4-19)...............................53

12. You Want Me To Do What? (Hosea 1:1-2:1).....................59

13. The Glory Of The Lord (Ezekiel 1:1-28)...........................67

14. A Barren Woman (Luke 1:5-7, 39-45, 57-60)....................73

15. A Righteous Man (Matthew 1:18-25)...............................78

16. The Common Man (Luke 2:8-20).....................................83

17. The Eyes Of Faith (Luke 2:21-35)....................................88

18. An Old Woman And A Young Baby (Luke 2:36-40)...........94

19. God In Her Womb (Luke 1:39-56)...................................98

20. Blinded, So That He Could See (Acts 9:1-19)...................102

21. Do Not Be Afraid! (Revelation 1: 9-20)...........................108

22. In Various Ways...112

Encounters With God

There was a time when mankind thought that the Milky Way Galaxy was all there was to the universe. Now scientists figure that there are more than one hundred billion (100,000,000,000) galaxies in the universe. Since our galaxy has over two hundred billion (200,000,000,000) stars itself, this should give you a picture of the number of stars in the universe and I have rounded my numbers down. The psalmist David, of course, did not know these numbers, but he did have an idea of the immensity of the heavens. That is why he wrote Psalm 8:3, 4 "When I consider your heavens, the work of your fingers, the moon and the stars which you have set in place, what is man that you are mindful of him, the son of man that you care for him?" When we consider the vastness of the universe, Earth seems to be such a tiny speck in it and we appear to be just puny creatures. Why indeed is God so concerned about us when we are only a small part of his incredible universe?

Isaiah 40:26 says, "Lift your eyes and look to the heavens: Who created all these? He brings out the starry host, one by one, and calls each by name. Because of his great power and mighty strength, not one of them is missing." Just imagine trying to individually name one hundred billion times two hundred billion stars. I tried typing in the calculation on a calculator, but it could not calculate such a high number. Obviously the God who created all of these stars must be beyond our comprehension. God himself declared in Isaiah 55:9, "As the heavens are higher than the earth, so are my ways higher than your ways and my thoughts higher than your thoughts." Our finite minds cannot grasp the infinite majesty of God. The only way that we can possibly know anything about God at all is for him to reveal himself to us. Fortunately, he has done so in several ways. Because he wants to have a relationship with us, he has condescended to meet us at our level so that in some way we can get to know him. This knowledge is, of course, fragmentary and incomplete on this side of eternity.

Throughout history many people have encountered God in many different ways. God has revealed himself to his people in dreams and visions. A theophany is a manifestation of God that is tangible to the human senses. Some would restrict it to a visible appearance of God while others would admit audible theophanies. The term comes from the Greek and literally means appearance of God. It has been applied to the appearance of the gods in Near Eastern religions and ancient Greek religions, but we will not use it in that sense here.

Theophanies in the Bible are relatively rare. Actually, it is indeed dangerous to be confronted by God. God said to Moses in Exodus 33:20, "You cannot see my face, for no one can see me and live." Hebrews 12:9 says, "For our God is a consuming fire." That is why it is not surprising that often the first words that a messenger from God says to a person is "Fear not." Theophanies tend to be sudden and dramatic. God appears and disappears without any notice. If he takes on a recognizable form at all, it is that of a human male; otherwise, he appears in a bush or a cloud or a breeze.

In this book I will be dealing with several individuals who encountered God. Some of them experienced a genuine theophany. Some of them did not. However, each of them did have a sudden and dramatic encounter with God. God surprised them with a visit. In most cases, the visit was very brief. Most of the stories will be from the Old Testament, but I have included a few from the New Testament.

I have decided not to include any stories from the life of Jesus while he walked this Earth. While some have referred to his life as one long theophany, most do not. Jesus lived amongst his people for some 33 years, which is hardly a sudden and dramatic appearance. In any case the stories of people encountering Jesus would fill a book, if not several books, on their own.

However, I have included a few stories of people encountering Jesus in the womb and as a baby. Their encounters are fascinating studies for us. It is one thing to meet God in a burning bush, but a womb or a manger! I have also included a couple of post-resurrection appearances of Jesus.

These stories are all fascinating stories. They deal with men and women who meet God and have their lives profoundly changed. Some are called to some special service. Some go back to their normal lives, but none remain unaffected by the experience. To meet God is to be changed by him.

In each of these encounters, God reveals a little about himself. Therefore, if we pay attention, we can learn a little more about him with each story. By carefully studying each encounter, we can gain some knowledge about God and about ourselves.

I have entitled this book *Take off Your Shoes* because in two of the encounters with God, God tells the person whom he encounters (Moses and Joshua) to take off his sandals because the ground on which he is standing is holy ground (Exodus 3:5; Joshua 5:15). The very immanent presence of God renders any place, no matter where it is, holy ground.

Not too long ago, on one of my visits to Fort Edmonton Park, I toured an old Muslim mosque. I was asked to take off my shoes on entering the building, which I did. One young woman who came in behind me objected and asked why we had to do so. I replied that we did this out of respect. As should be obvious since I am writing this book, I am not a Muslim. However, I felt that it was my duty to show respect for their building which they held sacred.

Unfortunately, Christians do not show the same respect when they enter the buildings where they worship God. I have often been a bi-vocational pastor and one of my jobs has been working as a church caretaker. Actually I have several years experience as a church caretaker and I have seen that some people show little respect for the building where they worship God. Not only do they not take off their shoes (which I do not expect), they do not even wipe their feet. Other people are so noisy in their conversations that people find it difficult to pray before or after the service. Where is the sense of reverence? Are we there to meet with God or to chat with friends? Are we there to worship, or just visit?

There is a definite contrast between how God can be approached before the cross of Jesus Christ and after. In the Old Testament, only the high priest could enter the Most Holy Place once a year on the Day of Atonement. Now that the veil of the temple has been torn in two from top to bottom, all who have confessed Jesus Christ as Lord and Saviour can come boldly into the presence of God. The high priest had a rope tied to his foot and bells on him so that the people could tell if God was not happy with his service and pull him out when God struck him dead. We are called to approach the throne of grace with confidence (Hebrews 4:16), but does that mean that we approach his presence casually? Even John, the disciple whom Jesus loved, did not take a casual approach when Jesus met him on the Isle of Patmos. Remember that John was one of the inner three and probably the one disciple who was the closest to Jesus. Yet when the risen Christ met him John says in Revelation 1:17, "When I saw him, I fell at his feet as though dead."

Chapter 1
Where Are You?
(Genesis 3:1-9)

This passage is a very familiar one. Most Christians know it very well. However, not everyone views this passage in the same way. Liberal scholars and non-Christians have questioned its historicity for at least a couple of centuries. Lately, even some Christians who might be called evangelicals have questioned it as well. With the general acceptance of the theory of evolution as the explanation of the origin of mankind, the idea of a literal Adam and Eve has come into disrepute. However, the study of genetics has led scientists to the discovery of a common link for all mankind. They say that we have all descended from a common ancestor who they name Eve. This, of course, does not prove the historicity of the Genesis account, but it does give it some credence. Many attempts have been made to reconcile the biblical account of creation with the theory of evolution, but I will not deal with them at this time. Suffice it to say that there are sincere Christians who accept evolution and educated scientists who believe in the biblical account of creation.

Paul, in Romans 5, clearly treats the account of the fall of mankind in Genesis 3 as history. He said in verse twelve, "Therefore, just as sin entered the world through one man, and death through sin, and in this way death came to all men, because all sinned." In verse 19 he said, "For just as through the disobedience of the one man the many were made sinners, so also through the obedience of the one man the many will be made righteous." As Christians, we would certainly not call into question the last half of this verse. We readily confess the belief that we are made righteous through our faith in Jesus Christ, the obedient One, who sacrificed himself for the many disobedient ones. How can we affirm our faith in the second Adam and yet disbelieve in the first? Frankly, I do not know. I do know that the Bible, and not just Genesis, treats the fall of man into sin as an historical event that happened at a point in time and not just some myth written to explain why we are sinners. In Luke's gospel, Jesus' ancestry is traced back to Adam.

Man's fall into sin is at the heart of the gospel. We are all sinners. We sinned in Adam and we inherited a tendency to sin from him. Therefore, we all sin. We all fall short of the glory of God (Romans 3:23). There are those that believe in the basic goodness of mankind, but they are deluded. Certainly, some people do noble and generous deeds, but that is not the whole story. Some people also commit genocide. We all have wicked, sinful thoughts. Some of us have the self-control not to put those thoughts into actions, but the thoughts are there nonetheless. Remember, that Jesus in Matthew 5:22 and 28 said that the thoughts themselves are sin even if they are never acted upon. Evil is resident in every human heart. Even the great apostle Paul admitted, in Romans 7, that he struggled with sin. Because we all are sinners, we need salvation. That is why Jesus Christ came to live and to die for us. Romans 5:8 says, "But God demonstrates his own love for us in this: While we were still sinners, Christ died for us."

Let us look at this story in Genesis. Let us examine the biblical account of mankind's fall into sin. It is an interesting story and a worthwhile study. If the fall of man is at the heart of the gospel, then we should know what the story is all about. Some may question the historicity of the details, but we must affirm that, at some point, mankind fell into sin. What exactly did happen in the Garden of Eden?

Genesis 1:27 says, "So God created man in his own image, in the image of God he created him; male and female he created them." This verse clearly states that mankind, both male and female, was created in the image of God. What does this mean? I remember that, as part of my ordination paper that I was preparing in seminary, I was asked to explain what I thought the image of God in mankind was. There are many explanations. Basically what this verse means is that people were especially created by God to be different from the animals and somehow like God. I remember when we had a cat named Alex. I got him for our daughter, Elizabeth, one Boxing Day. He was a beautiful white cat, but he was not very friendly. For some reason, though, he did like me. As a responsible pet owner, at the appropriate time, I took him to a clinic for the operation that I will not describe in detail now. When I came to pick him up, he recognized my voice and responded. Someone at the clinic made a comment about him recognizing his daddy and I was deeply offended, but kept my mouth shut. As much as I liked Alex, he was only a pet and not a child. In fact, he was a present for my child. People are different from animals and somehow like God. We were created to have dominion over the animals (verse 28). Obviously, that does not mean that we should abuse them in any way, but we are not to treat them as equals.

God created people to have fellowship with him. For a time that fellowship was good. Genesis 2:25 says, "The man and his wife were both naked, and they felt no shame." This means that they were created innocent, without sin. Thus, there was no sin barrier between them and God. We do not know how long this fellowship remained that way, but it must have been good. God gave man the task of taking care of the garden (2:15). He also gave him one command. He said in Genesis 2:17, "You must not eat from the tree of the knowledge of good and evil, for when you eat of it you will surely die." God put plenty of trees in the garden, but there were only two trees of consequence. Genesis 2:9 mentions those two trees. They were the tree of life and the tree of knowledge of good and evil. These trees represented the choice that man had. He could choose between life and death, between obedience and disobedience. God did not create us as sinful, but he did give us a choice to sin. There have been some who have questioned why he gave us that choice. Why did he not create us so that we could not sin? The answer to that question is quite simple. God did not want to create robots, but individuals with a free will. That is why I prefer cats as pets rather than dogs, although, at the present, I have neither. Cats are more independent. They do not need you in the same sense that dogs do. They can take care of themselves. Therefore, when they hang around you, it is because, in a limited sense, they choose to. That is a partial explanation of why God created us. He wanted people who would choose to have fellowship with him.

That is why he gave us the choice. We could choose the path of obedience and fellowship. We could choose the tree of life and live forever in submission to God. We could also choose the path of disobedience and rebellion. We could choose the tree of the knowledge of good and evil and die the death of independence. Of course, the forbidden was given its full appeal. "The tree was good for food and pleasing to the eye, and also desirable for gaining wisdom" (3:6). In order for the choice to be real, it had to be tempting. It had to be ice cream and not broccoli. I am not that fond of broccoli.

God gave us limits, but plenty of freedom within those limits. Only one tree was forbidden. These limits were good and not arbitrary. God still puts limits on mankind. He still wants us to live a life of dependence and submission. However, we often still choose the path of independence and rebellion.

Because there was no evil within mankind at the beginning, the temptation had to come from without. The tempter took the form of a serpent. Revelation 12:9 identifies him as the devil or Satan. He used deception to lead Eve astray and he has been deceiving people ever since. In John 8:44 Jesus said of Satan, "When he lies, he speaks his native language, for he is a liar and the father of lies." He began his path of deception with a question about the goodness of God. He questioned the limits that God had placed on man and appealed to Eve's spirit of independence right from the beginning. God, of course, had allowed mankind to eat from any tree but one and Satan questioned whether they could eat from any tree at all. Satan still tries to make God's commands sound arbitrary and harsh rather than normal and natural. He still exaggerates God's demands upon us. Eve responded by saying that she was indeed free to eat from any tree but one. However, even at first you can see her adding to the prohibition of God. God's original command only applied to eating the fruit of the tree. There was no mention of touching the tree. She had already joined Satan in magnifying God's strictness. She was already on the path to independence and ruin.

Next Satan introduces an outright lie. He says, "You will surely not die." He appeals to Eve's independence and pride by saying that she will be like God. Then Eve took that step of rebellion. She listened to Satan's deception and fell into his trap. The fruit was appealing. The offer of knowledge and wisdom was desirable. She did want to become like God. "She took some and ate it (verse 7). It seems like such a simple act, but it had profound implications. As I have already mentioned, Paul dealt with the implications of this initial disobedience in Romans 5. She also gave some to Adam and he ate it as well. Adam and Eve chose the path of independence and rebellion. They chose to disobey an explicit command of God. There was no excuse. They knew the command of God and chose instead to disobey it. They had been sold a false idea of evil as something beyond good. They had bought the idea that they were on a path to wisdom and sophistication rather than ruin and destruction.

There was some truth to what Satan said. Their eyes were opened, but they did not like what they saw. Their innocence was destroyed and could never be recovered. They saw their nakedness. Their sin was exposed and they tried to cover it. They were now condemned to death. Death did not come immediately, but it did come. If they had not eaten of the tree of knowledge of good and evil, then they could have stayed in the garden and eaten of the tree of life and lived forever, but because of their sin, they were driven out (verses 22-24). The sentence of death was upon them and upon all mankind because of their disobedience (Romans 5:12).

They tried to hide their sin. Not only did they cover themselves, but they also tried to hide from God. They tried to run from the consequences of what they had done. We still try to hide our sins. We still try to cover our wickedness.

Adam and Eve had been in intimate fellowship with God. They had enjoyed his presence, but now everything had changed. The fellowship that they enjoyed, they now shunned. They had destroyed the relationship that they had through their disobedience. It was not only the relationship with God that was affected. Their relationship with one another was marred as well. When Adam was confronted by God with his sin, he blamed Eve for leading him astray. He refused to take full responsibility for his sinful action. This pattern, as we all know, continues today. We still blame others for our failure and sin.

When Adam and Eve tried to hide, God called out, "Where are you?" (verse 9). Obviously, God is omniscient and omnipresent. He knew exactly where they were. This question is a confrontation, but a gentle one. God meant to draw them out of hiding rather than drive them out of hiding. God took the initiative to restore the fellowship, but still left it up to Adam and Eve to respond to that initiative. Right from the beginning, God sought out man. He is still seeking us out, trying to draw us out of our hiding places, gently confronting us.

The psalmist David knew that he could not hide from God. He said in Psalm 139:7, "Where can I go from your Spirit? Where can I flee from your presence?" He too had tried to cover his sin, but found that this was painful (Psalm 32:3-5). We still try to hide from God and people will continue to do so right up to the end. Revelation 6:16, 17 talks about the end times. It says: "They called to the mountains and the rocks, 'Fall on us and hide us from the face of him who sits on the throne and from the wrath of the Lamb! For the great day of their wrath has come, and who can stand?" For those who continue in their sin, the presence of God is a dreadful thing and they will always try to hide.

The presence of God can be a beautiful thing. It was beautiful for Adam and Eve before they fell into sin. It can be beautiful for us again. God still takes the initiative to restore the relationship with him. He actually planned for the redemption of man, for the reconciliation of our fellowship with him right from the beginning. In Revelation 13:8, Jesus is called the Lamb of God slain from the creation of the world." God knew that we would fall into sin and so he set a plan in place right from the beginning. He decided to send his Son to live and to die for us. He knew that we would destroy the fellowship that we had with him and with one another, so he provided a way to restore that fellowship.

As Paul said in Romans 5, we all sinned in Adam and, therefore, we all die. However, through the second Adam, Jesus Christ, we can all live. He paid the price of our redemption. He paid the debt of our sin. He provided the way for our reconciliation. He took the initiative. However, we must still respond. We must still repent of our sins and confess Jesus as our Lord. If we continue in our stubborn independence, then we are condemned to death. If we try to hide our sins, then God will find us and send his wrath upon us.

Adam and Eve had a wonderful fellowship with God. They destroyed their fellowship through independence and rebellion. However, God took the initiative to restore that fellowship. He sought them out and provided a way of reconciliation. Ultimately that reconciliation, that restoration, cost him the death of his Son on the cross of Calvary. We now can have the fellowship restored through his death and our faith in him if we repent of our sins and confess Jesus as our Lord. What choice have you made? Have you chosen independence and rebellion or repentance and faith?

Chapter 2
Questions and Answers
(Job 38-41)

The story of Job is well known, but often misunderstood. It is a story of a *righteous* sufferer. Many attempts have been made over the centuries to justify the suffering that Job endured calling him either proud or self-righteous. They must deal with God's verdict. Job 1:8 says, "then the LORD said to Satan, 'Have you considered my servant Job? There is no one on earth like him; he is blameless and upright, a man who fears God and shuns evil.'" After Satan took away all Job's possessions and family, Job still held to his faith in God. He fell to his face in worship and said, "Naked I came from my mother's womb and naked I will depart. The LORD gave and the LORD has taken away; may the name of the LORD be praised." (Job 1:21). After this trial, Satan again came before God. Job 2:3 says "Then the LORD said to Satan, 'Have you considered my servant Job? There is no one on earth like him; he is blameless and upright, a man who fears God and shuns evil. And he still maintains his integrity, though you incited me against him to ruin him without any reason.'" Note that God said, "without any reason." God said that Job did not deserve the suffering that he endured at the hand of Satan. Anyone who says that Job deserved his suffering is arguing against God.

At first Job's three friends Eliphaz, Bildad and Zophar came to comfort him. Indeed, they sat on the ground with him for seven days and seven nights. Ultimately, however, they all came to the conclusion that he must have done something to deserve the suffering that he was enduring and they all urged him to confess his sins before God. Chapters 3 to 31 contain beautiful poetry. In them we find a series of speeches back and forth between Job and his three friends. Job argued that he was righteous and his friends argued that he was a horrible sinner. Job argued that God has punished him unjustly and his friends argued that God is always just. In the midst of all of this debate, Job longed for God to speak or for someone to intervene on his behalf. It is the silence of God that is the most painful trial for Job to endure. In all of his speeches, that is his most common complaint, and not the loss of his wealth or even the loss of his family. Job says in Job 29:4, "Oh, for the days when I was in my prime, when God's intimate friendship blessed my house."

Job cannot understand why he is suffering. He has served God all his life and has never wandered away from him. He has many questions and he cries them out in his pain. Here is a sample of some of them: "If I have sinned, what have I done to you, O watcher of men? Why have you made me your target? Have I become a burden to you?" (7:20). "Why do you hide your face and consider me your enemy?" (13:24). "Why does the Almighty not set times for judgement? Why must those who know him look in vain for such days?" (24:1).

Job also listened to a long speech from Elihu. Although some have said that Elihu's speech, particularly the last part, is full of insight, I feel that the best comment on his speech is his own words in Job 32:18, "For I am full of words... " For the most part, Elihu's speech repeats what everyone else has already said, and he drones on and on. His speech is by far the most long and boring speech in the book. It is significant that God makes no comment whatsoever about his speech. God endorses what Job has said and condemns what Job's three friends have said, but says nothing about what Elihu has said. Perhaps this is because Elihu said nothing. However, the latter part of his speech does seem to prepare us for what follows. His description of God's coming in power is a bridge to God answering Job out of the storm.

After a long debate between Job and his three friends and a long and boring speech by Elihu, God finally answered Job. Job has longed for an answer to his many questions. God had been silent while Job suffered much pain and abuse and now God finally speaks. God's speeches in chapters 38 to 41 are addressed exclusively to Job. Although the others must still be present, God does not speak to them until he finishes admonishing Job and then he talks only to Eliphaz.

In Job 31:35 Job said, "I sign now my defence – let the Almighty answer me; let my accuser put his indictment in writing." Job had asked for a response from God and it finally came, but it was not the response that he wanted. He wanted a bill of indictment. He wanted a list of the charges against him so that he could answer them. He never received such a list. He wanted a verdict which he was confident would be a verdict of innocence. He never received a verdict. As a matter of fact, God's answer to Job does not appear to be an answer at all. In fact, it appears to be a series of questions.

God's two lengthy speeches to Job do not seem to address the issue of why Job was suffering even though he was righteous and in a right relationship with God. God never mentioned his wager with Satan. In fact, God made very few positive declarations. He answered Job's questions with questions. Job's friends came forward with a suggested list of Job's sins. God did not come forward with any list because it was not needed. Job had waited a long time for God to speak and God had spoken. The very fact that God spoke to him was enough for him. What God said was not as important as the fact that the relationship was restored. Everything was all right between himself and God. Knowing that, nothing else matters. Whatever happens to him is unimportant compared to that.

Job was at first rebuked for speaking without knowledge. However, this is a limitation that we all deal with – speaking without knowledge. Only God knows everything. Behind the grandeur of the questions that God hammers at Job was the implication that Job must accept his limitations. Job did not understand how the universe functions and he never would. God was infinitely beyond his grasp and he must acknowledge that. Amazingly, Job did respond positively to God's barrage of questions. Job did repent. It was enough for him that God had spoken.

Because Job never really got a straight answer to his questions, neither do we. Indeed, the central issue of why the righteous suffer is never really settled in the Bible. We do not know how old the book of Job is. The guesses vary by hundreds of years. However, we do have an idea as to when Job lived and that was a very long time ago. That fact is important. Job lived before any of the Bible was written. He lived long before Moses and the prophets and certainly long before Jesus. Job maintained his faith in God when Satan took away his wealth, his family and his health. He trusted in him without any of the supports that we take for granted today. We look back on a long line of heroes of faith that trusted in God to bolster our faith. Some of that long line is recorded in Hebrews 11. Job did not have that long line. We have the church to support us in our relationship with God. Job did not have the church or even a priestly class. We have the entire Bible to read. None of it was written at the time of Job. The prophets have revealed much about God to us. The prophets all came hundreds of years after the time of Job. We have family to lean on in times of stress. Satan took Job's family away from him. Job's wife told him to curse God and die. We have friends to console us when times are tough. Job's friends turned on him and accused him of sin. Job trusted in God when Satan pulled all of the supports out from under him. He maintained his faith even when his experience told him otherwise. Here is the proof that a person can love God simply for who he is without a thought of receiving a reward.

I entitled this chapter "Questions and Answers" because the book of Job is all about questions and answers. It is particularly appropriate because God answered Job's questions with more questions. These questions are the only answers that Job needed to his questions. The Bible does not answer all our questions because it cannot. We would not understand the answers. Like Job, our minds are finite and God's mind is infinite. As Isaiah 55:8, 9 says, "'For my thoughts are not your thoughts, neither are your ways my ways,' declares the LORD. 'As the heavens are higher than the earth, so are my ways higher than your ways and my thoughts than your thoughts.'" Some of our questions must always remain unanswered, at least for now. As the apostle Paul put it in 1 Corinthians 13:12, "Now we see but a poor reflection as in a mirror; then we shall see face to face. Now I know in part; then I shall know fully even as I am fully known."

Chapter 3
Is Anything too Hard for the LORD?
(Genesis 18:1-5)

In this chapter we are studying one of the several appearances of God to Abraham. Abraham was a specially chosen servant of God. God called him out of his homeland and away from his family and Abraham followed God. God promised to bless him and make him into a great nation. Abraham was called the "Friend of God". James 2:23 says, "And the scripture was fulfilled that says, 'Abraham believed God, and it was credited to him as righteousness,' and he was called God's friend."

Abraham is remembered for his faith in God. He left the security of home to venture into the unknown because God had called him. He believed God's promises even when it looked like they could not possibly be fulfilled. Paul talked about Abraham's faith in Romans 4:16-22.

There are several things that are unusual about this appearance of God. One is that God appeared to Abraham in the form of a man and ate with him. Another is that he was accompanied by two companions. These two were later shown to be angels. Because God appeared to Abraham in human form, he did not recognize him at first.

Abraham was sitting at the entrance to his tent when God appeared to him. This is because it was the hottest part of the day. Anyone familiar with the conditions in that part of the world would know that it is difficult to do anything in such heat and there was no air conditioning then. One normally seeks shade at such times and rests until it cools off. The practice of an afternoon siesta at such times is still practised in some hot countries today. Thus, Abraham was very prudent to be resting in the shade of his tent at that time. However, the visitors who came along did not seem to be as prudent. It was decidedly unusual for anyone to travel in the midday sun. Abraham probably wondered, "Why are they so foolish and what are they doing here?"

Most people would have been apprehensive when they were faced with such an unusual situation. Yet Abraham was not. It is interesting to reflect on what his attitude was at that time and the attitudes of the rest of those involved as well.

When Abraham saw three strangers approaching him in the heat of the day he might have been frightened and called his servants to arms, but he was not. He might have been angry with them for interrupting his afternoon rest, but he was not. Indeed, Abraham was a very gracious host. He did all he could to make these strangers welcome and comfortable.

In fact, Abraham did more than what was really necessary. He picked out a choice calf when another might have been good enough. He had his wife, Sarah, bake more bread than was necessary. He asked her to get 20 quarts of flour. Instead of sitting and eating with the visitors, he stood nearby under a tree. Abraham was more than hospitable. Also, we must remember that it was the hottest part of the day. Thus, these elaborate preparations must have been difficult for Abraham, Sarah and their servants.

Hospitality has always been important in that part of the world. The almost royal honours paid to a chance visitor, the fervent welcome, however inconvenient the moment, the assurance that his arrival was an honour, even a providence, and the lavish meal called only a morsel of bread are still characteristic of Bedouin hospitality. Note that Lot was also a gracious host to his two visitors. This visit is recorded in Genesis 19. Our fear and distrust of strangers is most unfortunate. Abraham and Lot did not know who they were entertaining, but they were gracious anyway.

The importance of hospitality is stressed in scripture. Hebrews 13:2 says, "Do not forget to entertain strangers, for by so doing some people have entertained angels without knowing it." Jesus said that when we show hospitality to others, we are doing it for him. He said in Matthew 25:35, "For I was hungry and you gave me something to eat, I was thirsty and you gave me something to drink, I was a stranger and you invited me in." Do you remember the punishment meted out to those who did not show hospitality? This admonition should motivate us to show hospitality to strangers and to others. Hospitality was also one of the requirements for church officers listed by Paul to Titus. Titus 1:8 says, "Rather he must be hospitable, one who loves what is good, who is self-controlled, upright, holy and disciplined." Scripture is abundantly clear on the importance of hospitality. It is a vital ingredient in demonstrating our faith in and our love for Jesus.

As I mentioned before, this was not God's first appearance to Abraham. He had appeared to him three times before. At each time, God had promised Abraham that he would be a father. In Genesis 12:2, God promised to make a great nation out of Abraham. This promise obviously depended on Abraham having at least one son. In Genesis 15:4, God promised Abraham that his own son would be his heir. Genesis 17:19

says, "Then God said, 'Yes, but your wife Sarah will bear a son, and you will call him Isaac. I will establish my covenant with him as an everlasting covenant for his descendants after him.'" Yes, God made it clear to Abraham that he was going to have a son in his old age.

Why did God visit Abraham again with the same promise? The visits of chapters 17 and 18 must have been close together since, in both cases, the son is promised within a year. Did Abraham's faith need a further boost from God? No, by now, Abraham believed God's promise. This visit was not for Abraham's sake, but for Sarah's.

Sarah was not with Abraham when God promised him that he would have a son by her. Also, Abraham had either not told her about God's promise or he had failed to convince her. In any case, she was not anticipating becoming a mother and God had to prepare her for that. Note that Abraham was asked about his wife in verse nine. Note also that verse ten mentions that Sarah was listening at the tent door. Since tent walls were by no means sound proof, she must have heard every word that was said. God, though he was addressing Abraham, was actually speaking to Sarah and promising her a son in her old age.

Sarah was, of course, to be an instrument in fulfilling God's promise. Since God had chosen her for a task, he had to prepare her for that task. Each time God promised Abraham a son, the promise became more specific. God kept moving toward its fulfilment and Sarah was to be a part of that fulfilment.

What God was promising Sarah was undoubtedly a miracle. We learn from Genesis 17:17 that Abraham was one hundred years old and Sarah was ninety when Isaac was born to them. It was impossible for them to have a child at that age. God had to work a miracle of regeneration in Sarah to restore her youth. Genesis 18:18 makes it clear that Sarah was well past child bearing age. Physically speaking, there was no way that she could have a child. Yet God specializes in the impossible. Sarah's barrenness and old age was no barrier to him. He would keep his promise despite the obstacles in the way.

When God appeared to Abraham and told him that Sarah would bear him a son, he laughed. Genesis 17:17 says, "Abraham fell face down; he laughed and said to himself, 'Will a son be born to man a hundred years old? Will Sarah bear a child at the age of ninety?'" It had seemed incredible to him at first, but Abraham came to believe God and kept his covenant of circumcision to demonstrate his belief.

When Sarah heard God's promise, she laughed as well. That is why Isaac was given his name. Isaac means, "He laughs." His very name would be for Abraham and Sarah a reminder of the incredible nature of his birth.

Sarah just could not believe that she would have a son. She thought that she was old and worn out. She had wanted a son badly all of her married life, but she had given up hope. After all, when she was younger, there was still a possibility, but now it was impossible. She had passed the child bearing stage of life a long time ago.

Sarah was confronted by God about her unbelief. God said in verse 13, "Why did Sarah laugh and say, 'Will I really have a child, now that I am old?'" Sarah tried to deny that she had laughed because she was afraid, but God confronted her with her dishonesty as well. He assured her that, though the thing to be done was unusual, extraordinary, and unnatural, he could still accomplish it. He said, "Is anything too hard for the LORD?" Jeremiah 32:17 says, "Ah, Sovereign LORD, you have made the heavens and the earth by your great power and outstretched arm. Nothing is too hard for you." God can do anything. There is no limit to his power. Sarah had to learn that truth.

Sarah did learn that truth. She came to believe in the promise of God. She did bear a son and they named him Isaac.

It is not always easy to believe the promises of God. Often they seem impossible. Sarah was not the only one to have had her doubts. Mark 9 tells the story of a man who had a son who was demon possessed. He brought him to Jesus and asked for his help. Jesus said to him in verse 23, "Everything is possible for him who believes." The man replied, "I do believe; help me overcome my unbelief." His faith needed bolstering, but Jesus did cast the demon out of his son. God often goes to great lengths to bolster the faith of those who believe in him. Do you remember the story of Gideon and his fleece?

God's incredible power has been demonstrated time and time again. There is nothing that he cannot do. He can do things that we cannot even imagine. Ephesians 3:20 says, "Now to him who is able to do immeasurably more than all we ask or imagine, according to the power that is at work within us... "

We must believe in God's power to do the impossible. Hebrews 11:6 says, "And without faith it is impossible to please God, because anyone who comes to him must believe he exists and that he rewards those who earnestly seek him." Faith is an essential prerequisite of our salvation. John 3:18 says, "Whoever believes in him is not condemned, but whoever does not believe stands condemned already because he has not believed in the name of God's one and only Son." John 3:36 says the same thing in different words.

Yet most people say that they believe in God. This belief is not enough. James 2:19 says, "You believe that there is one God. Good! Even the demons believe that – and shudder." Our faith must be demonstrated by our actions. We must step out in faith. We may believe that a bridge will hold us, but until we walk across the bridge, we have not shown faith. In order to find salvation and to grow in Christ, we must have faith. We must put ourselves totally in God's control. We cannot hold anything back. God is willing to bolster our faith, but he demands that we exercise it.

Chapter 4
Your Only Son
(Genesis 22:1-19)

We have been looking at different encounters with God in the Old Testament for several chapters now. Last chapter, we examined Abraham's encounter with God and two angels. Let us return to Abraham and look at another encounter. Abraham was a man of faith. He had left his country and his family to go to a strange land because God had called him and promised to bless him. Part of the blessing was a son. That promise was not fulfilled for many years. Abraham was one hundred years old and his wife Sarah was ninety when Isaac was finally born to them.

This long wait was one test of Abraham's faith. In this passage we see another test. In fact, this was Abraham's greatest test. In this chapter, we see Abraham's character revealed and get another glimpse of what God is like. Each separate encounter with God that we look at shows us another aspect of God. This was a momentous occasion in the life of Abraham, an eventful time.

In verse one we see the purpose behind this significant occasion in Abraham's life. It says, "God tested Abraham." The King James Version is somewhat misleading for it uses the word "tempted" instead of "tested". Yet we know from James 1:13 that God does not tempt anyone. It is not a tempting to sin that is described here, but a testing that would reveal Abraham's faith as nothing else had done. He was called to give evidence of his absolute obedience and unquestioning trust in God.

No test could have been more severe. Abraham's trust was weighed in the balance against common sense, human affection and lifelong ambition. Abraham was told to sacrifice his son, Isaac. In the Hebrew there is more of an emphasis on the fact that Isaac was his only son. We know from Genesis 16, however, that Abraham had a son earlier by his wife's maidservant, Hagar. This son was named Ishmael. He was not the child of promise and he was sent away when Isaac was born. Thus, in a sense, Isaac was Abraham's only son.

Abraham was asked to offer up Isaac as a burnt offering. A burnt offering meant the complete dedication and total sacrifice of the victim. Abraham was asked to prove that he loved God more than he loved his son although his son was very special to him. The demand seemed totally unreasonable. Murder was expressly prohibited in Genesis 9:5, 6. In addition, God gave no reason for the sacrifice. Abraham was called to blind obedience.

All of us at one time or another will have our faith tested. There will be occasions when we will be asked to obey God when obedience seems foolish. We may be asked to choose between our love for our family and friends and our love for God. Luke 24:26 makes it very clear that our highest loyalty and deepest devotion must be directed to God and no one else.

When God called, Abraham responded promptly. He got an early start the next morning and set off for the place that God had sent him to. The early start showed his resoluteness in facing the test that God had given him. He found no excuses for delay. The journey took three days so there was plenty of time to reconsider, but he did not change his mind. He passed through the fiercest fires, stood up under the mightiest pressure and endured the most difficult strain.

Abraham carried out all of the necessary steps. He made the long journey. He brought the wood, the fire and the knife. He built the altar, bound up his son, Isaac, and placed him on the altar. Abraham's test was not one isolated act of allegiance, but a three day ordeal of many steps. Think of how Abraham must have felt as he journeyed to Moriah with his son, Isaac. No obedience could have been more perfect than Abraham's.

Abraham told no one about God's demand and he separated himself from everyone so that no one could interfere. He did not even tell Isaac what was going to happen to him. Yet Isaac became curious when he saw that his father brought no lamb with them and he questioned his father about it. Note that Isaac addressed Abraham as father and Abraham addressed Isaac as his son. This was another reminder to Abraham of the terrible deed that he was asked to perform.

Abraham's reply in verse eight can be seen as either evasive or a reply of faith, "God himself will provide the lamb for the burnt offering, my son." Note also what he said to his servants in verse five, "We will worship and then we will come back to you." He was confident that somehow he would return with Isaac. He had faith to see beyond the sacrifice. He trusted in God's promise to bless him through Isaac even though he was going to sacrifice him. This is made clear in Hebrews 11:17-19.

Abraham demonstrated both obedience and faith. That is why he is called the father of all who believe (Romans 4:16, 17). James 2:20-24 says that Abraham demonstrated his faith by his sacrifice of Isaac. This test proved that he had faith in God.

In the end, Abraham did not have to offer his son. God's command was only a trial. God did not want Isaac – only Abraham's faith and obedience (Micah 6:1-8). God had tried Abraham's heart and he was satisfied. God was pleased that Abraham was willing to obey him in everything.

God provided a ram for the sacrifice instead of Isaac. Abraham's words to Isaac in verse eight were fulfilled. His trust in God was vindicated. Abraham named the place "Jehovah Jireh" or "the LORD will provide". This was Abraham's attitude toward God. He trusted in God to provide for him.

After Abraham had confirmed his obedience and faith, God confirmed his blessing upon him. To obey is to find new assurance. When we step out in faith, God blesses us abundantly. He rewards us for our obedience. God confirmed his blessing upon Abraham with an oath. Hebrews 6:13-18 points out that this confirms the fact that God's promise to Abraham was secure and unchangeable.

God still blesses those who trust and obey. Yet there are few people like Abraham who are willing to give up what they hold dear in order to claim the promises of God. Isaac submitted to the sacrifice. Both he and his father, Abraham, were willing to trust and obey. This crisis made them shine forth as gold (1 Peter 1:7).

Abraham's words have greater significance in the light of the cross. God not only provided the ram that day, but he also provided the ultimate sacrifice – Jesus Christ, his only Son (Romans 8:32). Abraham's love for God mirrored God's greater love for us. His faith gave him a glimpse of the resurrection as Hebrews 11:17-19 shows us.

As 2 Chronicles 3:1 tells us, Moriah, where Abraham offered up Isaac, was also the place where God halted the plague on Israel when David sacrificed to him. It was also the place where Solomon built the temple, a place where sacrifices were offered to God. It was also in the vicinity of Calvary where God offered up his only Son for our sin.

God gave his best – his only Son. In return, he wants our best. He wants us to sacrifice all that we hold dear in order that we might serve him. He promised to bless us abundantly when we step out in faith for him.

Chapter 5
Wrestling With God
(Genesis 32:22-32)

This passage of scripture describes one of the most unusual encounters if not the most unusual in the whole Bible. The idea of God appearing in the form of a man and wrestling with Jacob would probably be rejected by us if it were not recorded in the Bible. It is especially difficult to conceive how it could be a long and close struggle, which is the way that it is clearly described. There are even some people who would refer to Jacob wrestling with an angel rather than with God. That would make it more reasonable to believe, but verse 28 plainly says that Jacob struggled with God.

To fully understand this passage, we must know the circumstances that led up to this momentous event in Jacob's life. Let us look at the story of Jacob's life up to this point. He was one of two sons born to Isaac. His twin brother, Esau, was born before him, but Jacob came out of the womb grasping Esau's heel. Before they were even born, God told Rebekah, their mother, "the older will serve the younger" (Genesis 25:23). Jacob tricked Esau into selling his rights as firstborn for a single meal. Also, he gained the blessing that was meant for Esau by deceiving his father Isaac. Because of these two deeds, Jacob fled to Paddan Aram to escape Esau's wrath. It was there that he met and fell in love with Rachel. He worked seven years for her father, Laban, to earn the right to marry her. However, Laban tricked him by giving him her older sister, Leah, instead. Then Jacob worked another seven years for Rachel. After that he worked another six years for Laban, but Laban kept changing his wages. Eventually, Jacob grew tired of Laban's treatment of him and snuck off one night with his family and possessions. Laban caught up to Jacob, but God warned him not to harm him so Laban let him go.

Now Jacob had another problem. He was free from his father-in-law, but what about his brother, Esau? Was Esau still angry with him? Would he try to kill him? Jacob was not sure. Twenty years is a long time, but some people can nurse a hatred for a lifetime.

Jacob felt helpless in this situation. He was very much afraid of Esau. His fear drove him to prayer. This prayer is recorded for us in verses nine to twelve. It was when Jacob realized his helplessness that God met him in his need. It was on the night before his encounter with Esau that he met the crucial test of his life. Jacob had a hunger for God that was awakened by the crisis that he faced and God came to satisfy that hunger. God intervened into his affairs to meet his needs when he came to God in prayer.

In this encounter with God, Jacob made some important discoveries. He learned some truths that would affect his life from that moment on.

Even though he knew that he was helpless in the situation, Jacob still tried to do what he could. He resorted to his usual craftiness to help him in his confrontation with Esau. His elaborate plans to appease his twin brother are recorded for us in verses 3 to 8 and 12 to 21. Jacob thought that a huge present might cool his brother's anger. Verse 20 says, "I will pacify him with these gifts I am sending on ahead; later, when I see him, perhaps he will receive me."

After Jacob had sent his gifts ahead toward Esau, he sent his family across the Jabbok. The Jabbok is a small tributary of the Jordan River. Whether Jacob sent his wives and children ahead to protect himself or whether he wanted to be alone to prepare himself for the coming crisis is not certain. In any case, by the time he actually met Esau, he went ahead of his family.

Whatever Jacob's reason for being alone was, it was all part of God's plan. In order to confront him, God wanted Jacob alone. God usually confronts us as individuals. We all must eventually face God alone. The best time for us to meet God and really get serious with him is when we are alone. That is why Jesus said in Matthew 5:5, 6 that we should seek a private place to pray. There is nothing wrong with public prayer as long as it is not made a spectacle for others to see. However, our deepest needs are best expressed to God in private. Also, the best time for God to speak to us is when we are alone. We must never neglect our private devotions. We cannot grow in our Christian life without spending time alone with God. What would our relationships with our spouses be like if we never spent time alone with them?

Jacob found himself in a very tough wrestling match. It took all night and it seemed that there was no clear victor. The identity of Jacob's assailant was not clear to him at first, but it became clear to him eventually. Jacob was given several clues and he was quick to seize each of them. The first clue was his opponent's ability to put his hip out of joint. We must remember that Jacob was a very strong and capable man. When he met Rachel, he rolled the stone away from the well, which was a task that normally took several men to accomplish. Thus, he should not have had too much trouble wrestling with an ordinary man. Also, a mere touch should not have put his hip out of joint. Therefore, Jacob knew that there was something unusual about his wrestling opponent. This is why he asked for a blessing. He was beginning to understand who he was struggling with. The further exchanges dispelled any doubts that he might have had. The man told Jacob that he had struggled with God and with man. Then Jacob asked him his name and he refused to give it. It was often thought that knowledge of a man's name gave you some magical power over him. Thus, Jacob's attempt to learn God's name was probably some effort to gain control over him. That is why God refused to tell him his name. We see a similar occurrence in Judges 13:16-18. Manoah wanted to learn God's name and God refused to reveal it.

It was when Jacob finally realized who he had been wrestling with that he came to understand that he had been struggling with God all of his life. This conflict brought to a head the battling and groping of a lifetime. His struggles with Esau and Laban were actually struggles with God.

Jacob's desperate embrace on his assailant vividly illustrated his ambivalent attitude toward God. He was both defiant toward him and dependent upon him. He had both been running away from God and running toward him. Jacob had been depending upon his own strength and cunning all his life. He wanted to make it on his own. It was only when he was faced with a situation wholly beyond his ability that he realized that he had to depend upon God.

All of us like to be independent. We like to think that we do not need anyone else. However, we do need others and we especially need God. Without him we can do nothing. This is a truth that we need to learn over and over again. We must stop trying to do things in our own strength and start depending on God to work through us. We want to make it through life on our own, but we cannot. We want to make it to heaven on our own, but we cannot. We want to earn our salvation by our good works, but we cannot. We need to depend wholly upon God. There is no other way. Jacob tried to be independent, but he came to realize the futility of such an attitude. He gave up his struggling and came to depend upon God. When Jacob realized that he had been struggling with God, he was amazed that his life had been spared. He wondered how he could encounter God face to face and live through the experience. He came to understand the depths of God's mercy toward him.

Jacob was probably the least worthy recipient of the blessing of God. He had violated the ethics of God's covenant with man. He was a deceiver and a scoundrel. His very name, Jacob, signified his character. Jacob means he who deceives or supplants. In declaring his name to God, he admitted what type of person he was. At that time, the person and the name were thought to be so inseparably bound together that to know a person's name was to know him in his very being.

Thus, when God gave Jacob a new name, it symbolized a new character. The changing of his name meant that he, himself, had changed. He was now destined to be a God governed man instead of an unscrupulous supplanter. Israel means "he strives with God." His new name was both a mark of grace, wiping out an old reproach, and an accolade to live up to. In his struggle with God, Jacob had come to realize God's power and had yielded himself to him. It was at the moment of yielding that he became a new man who could receive the blessing of God and become part of God's plan.

Jacob's struggle with God was very real. His limp would have been a perpetual reminder to him of the encounter. Jacob had both won and lost in the battle as Hosea 12:3, 4 points out. It was the defeat of the old man, Jacob, and his independent way of doing things – by cunning and deceit. It was the victory of the new man, Israel, and the new way of doing things – by depending upon God's resources. Before this encounter, Jacob could not meet the crisis that confronted him. Now he could. By realizing his own weakness, he gained the strength of God.

The apostle Paul realized this truth and said in 2 Corinthians 12:9, 10: "But he said to me, 'My grace is sufficient for you, for my power is made perfect in weakness,' Therefore I will boast all the more gladly about my weaknesses, so that Christ's power may rest on me. That is why, for Christ's sake, I delight in weaknesses, in insults, in hardships, in persecutions, in difficulties. For when I am weak, then I am strong." We must also come to that same conclusion. We must stop depending upon on our own strength and start depending on God.

All of us, if we are willing to admit it, have struggled with God at one time or another. We want to do things in our own strength and in our own way. We tend to put God out of the picture. We do not deny his authority, but we act as if he does not exist, or at least is not concerned about us. We carry out our plans as if we do not need God. However, sooner or later, we are faced with a problem that is beyond our limited capabilities. It may be the loss or sickness of a loved one. It may be a financial crisis like the loss of a job. It may be the loss of our own health. It may be the rejection of a friend or loved one. It may be any one of these things or may be several of them bearing down on us all at once. It is usually in such situations that we realize our need of God and come to him in prayer.

It is in the crises of life that God struggles with us to change us in order to make us face our problems as different people. We can only become new men and women when God wrestles down the old man or woman. It is at the point of yielding to God that we are equipped to meet the difficulties of life. However, we do not have to wait until a crisis comes into our life before we yield to God.

God desires to confront us all individually. All of us have areas of our life that we have not yet yielded fully to his control. Often God has to isolate us from our support structures and defences to make us realize who we are and who he is. Then he comes down to meet us in our areas of need. When God meets us, we can never be the same again. To come face to face with God is to be changed by God. That is the lesson that Jacob learned and that is what we must learn. We must stop trying to go it alone and turn our lives over to God. It is at the point of surrender that we win the victory.

Chapter 6
Who Am I?
(Exodus 3:1-14)

In this chapter we are examining God's initial encounter with Moses. It is different from his encounters with Abraham and Jacob. Moses is an interesting person to study. He was raised in luxury and educated in all the wisdom of Egypt as the son of Pharoah's daughter. He seemed destined for some high office. However, one day he went out to look at his fellow Israelites and saw an Egyptian beating one of them. He killed the Egyptian and hid the body, thinking that no one had seen him. Unfortunately for him, he was seen and he was forced to flee Egypt. He went to Midian where he met Jethro. He married Jethro's daughter, Zipporah, and ended up taking care of his sheep. One impulsive act had cost him a great deal. Moses had tried to redeem Israel in his own time and in his own way, and he had failed.

However, that failure was not final. God could still use Moses. He called him while he was out tending his father-in-law's flock. It is interesting to note that God usually calls people who are busy doing something. He seldom calls people who are sitting around waiting for his call. If you want to know God's will for your life, then get busy doing what the Bible calls you to do.

Moses' encounter with God at Mount Horeb, or Sinai as it is often called, was very significant. It was the turning point in his life and in Israel's history. It is interesting to study what took place that important day.

Moses was busy at his normal routine. It was a typical day in his life until he saw an incredible sight. He saw a bush burning in the desert and the bush was not being consumed by the fire. This, of course, aroused Moses' curiosity. He went over to the bush to find out what was going on. God used Moses' natural curiosity to draw him to the place where he wanted to meet with him. This is sometimes the way God works. He uses the spectacular and unusual to attract someone's attention.

Verse two says, "the angel of the LORD appeared to him". This term is often used in the Old Testament as a reverential synonym for the presence of God himself. Fire is also used frequently in the Old Testament as a sign of God's presence. It is also used as a symbol of God's holiness.

The holiness of God is definitely stressed here. It is interesting that this is the first mention of the adjective "holy" in the Bible. Holy means to be set apart, to be separate or different. Since God is totally set apart from his creation, anything associated with him or devoted to him becomes holy. Therefore, the ground where God met Moses became holy. The holiness of God is probably the most neglected truth in Christianity today. We tend to treat God too casually. We come into his presence without any thought of preparing ourselves to meet him. If we were meeting the Queen or the Prime Minister, then we would put on our best clothes and check the etiquette books to see how we should act. However, when we come to meet the King of Kings and Lord of Lords we are almost indifferent to his presence. Moses was commanded to take off his sandals as a sign of reverence and worship. This is a reminder to us that we are to show proper reverence for God when we come to worship him. We should also note that Moses hid his face because he was afraid to look at God.

Once God caught Moses' attention, he began to speak to him. At first what God said sounded good to Moses. God had seen the suffering of his people and he was about to deliver them. This was what Moses had wanted all along. He had been waiting forty years for this. The bondage of Moses' fellow Israelites was finally going to end. God had remembered his covenant with Abraham and was about to fulfill his promises.

However, while verses seven to nine sounded good to Moses, verse ten did not sound as good. Moses definitely wanted God to deliver his brethren, but he no longer wanted to be the agent of that deliverance. Forty years ago he was ready to intervene on behalf of his countrymen, but not now. His opinion of himself had changed dramatically. He was no longer full of self-confidence. After forty years as a humble shepherd he no longer felt like a deliverer.

Nevertheless, God did give the task to Moses. This was Moses' call into God's service and it was a definite call. There was no mistaking the fact that God himself was speaking to him and giving him a job to do. God wanted him and he wanted him now. Timing is very important to God. Moses had tried to run ahead of God by forty years and had failed because his timing was wrong. Now the timing was right. Moses had been too impatient, now he was too patient. Do we run ahead of God?

Moses was quite convinced that he was the wrong man for the job. His question, "Who am I?" is a clear indication of this. He could not understand why God had chosen him. While he had felt self-reliant in Egypt, he felt inadequate in Midian. Moses at 80 was not as eager to go against the Egyptians as he was when he was forty. However, God did not want him when he was full of self-confidence. God does not want people who think that they do not need him. He wants people to trust in him rather than themselves.

Moses had many excuses. He was afraid that the Israelites would not accept him as God's agent. He did not think that he was a good enough speaker. Basically he questioned why God had called him. He accused God of picking the wrong man. However, God never does that. It is obvious that Moses was reluctant to obey God's call, and all of his excuses were simply attempts at avoiding responsibility.

This is a very common problem in the church today. Many people are unwilling to accept the responsibilities that are given them and make excuses in order to duck these responsibilities. We must all examine ourselves to see if we are guilty of this.

God answered Moses' excuses with the promise that he would be with him (verse 12). Moses wanted to know God's name so that he could go before the Israelites. Basically Moses was asking for an indication of a new revelation since God reveals himself through his name. A new name means a new revelation. God reveals himself through his names. To know God's name is to know God at least in part.

The name that God gave Moses is a strange one. God said "I am whom I am. This is what you are to say to the Israelites: 'I AM has sent me to you.'" God declares his mysterious self existence in this name. This is clearly applicable to only God. God's name means "I am who I am" or "I will be who I will be". This is the special covenant name of God and has been pronounced Jehovah or Yahweh. This is the name under which God redeemed his people. The Israelites themselves refused to pronounce it, and thus the correct pronunciation has been lost. Probably Yahweh is closest. This is the only place in the Bible where God's covenant name is defined in any way.

God answered Moses' excuses in two ways. He promised him his presence and he gave him some signs as proof that he would be with him. This should have been good enough for anyone. What more could anyone want than God's powerful presence? When Jesus gave us his Great Commission in Matt.28:19, 20, he promised us his presence. It is the same promise that God gave Moses.

God caught Moses' attention and gave him a job to do. However, Moses felt inadequate to the task and made excuses. God answered these excuses by promising him his powerful presence. It is interesting that Moses asked God, "Who am I" and God's answer was basically, "I am who I am." This is to remind Moses, and us as well, that it is not who we are that counts, but who God is. When God gives us a job to do, we may think that we are old and washed up and useless like Moses, but that is not the issue. Who we are does not matter. God knows all of our limitations much better than we do. He is not concerned with them at all. Any excuse that we could dream up does not matter to God. He can do anything with anybody.

Chapter 7
Whose Side Are You On?
(Joshua 5:13-15)

We all want God to be on our side. This is by no means a new phenomenon. We thought that God was on our side in World War I and World War II. Bob Dylan even wrote a song called, "With God on Our Side". Jesus, God incarnate, also faced the issue of people wanting him to be on their side. Luke 12:13 says, "Someone in the crowd said to him, 'Teacher, tell my brother to divide the inheritance with me.'" Jesus' answer to him was quite definite, "Man, who appointed me a judge or an arbiter between you?" (verse 14). Jesus refused to take sides and used the occasion to warn against greed.

Sports teams and individual athletes have claimed that God was on their side and gave them the victory. I remember hearing about one athlete claiming that an unseen hand moved the football so that the opposing team missed the field goal and his team won the championship. Does God really intervene in such cases? Does he take sides in athletic contests? If he does, then how does he pick the winner? Devout Christians have been on the losing end in both wars and athletic contests.

In this passage in Joshua, Joshua encountered God and asked him, "Are you for us or for our enemies?" This was just another way of saying, "Whose side are you on?" Note God's answer, "Neither... " Joshua was preparing to attack Jericho and God was not on his side! Why was God not on his side? Let us look at this passage to find the answer to that question and its implications for today.

This encounter with God has some similarities with Moses and the burning bush (Exodus 3) and Jacob wrestling with God (Genesis 32). In all three cases the individual encounters God before he is about to face a life or death struggle. However, Joshua did not argue or wrestle with God. He simply questioned him and responded as he was told. Both Jacob and Moses wanted to avoid the coming conflict, but Joshua accepted and maybe even looked forward to it.

The man's drawn sword was very threatening. The burning bush was, at first, just a curiosity to Moses. Jacob did not know the identity of his wrestling opponent at first and would have mistaken him for an ordinary human being. Thus, the threat to Jacob appeared to be the greatest and would have prompted his question. The reply, "but as commander of the army of the LORD I now have come" (verse 14) made him fall prostrate to the ground. This is a sign of profound reverence.

There are several indicators that this is a genuine theophany, an explicit appearance of God. The man identified himself as commander of the LORD's army. This is a definite role of divine authority. Joshua fell face down before him in reverent worship and he accepted his worship. When John fell down at the feet of an angel to worship him, he was told to worship God alone. Revelation 19:10 says, "At this I fell at his feet to worship him. But he said to me, 'Do not do it! I am a fellow servant with you and with your brothers who hold to the testimony of Jesus. Worship God! For the testimony of Jesus is the spirit of prophecy.'" Joshua was told to take off his sandals because the place where he was standing is holy. This should remind us of God's word to Moses in Exodus 3. The place was holy because it was where God met his chosen leader in a special way. A further indication that this is a genuine theophany is the instructions given by God to Joshua in chapter six. God appeared to Joshua to prepare him for the task ahead and to instruct him as to how he was to go about it. He also came to reassure him.

Joshua was confronted by a man with a drawn sword and naturally wanted to know whose side he was on. The man's weapon showed that he was not one to be toyed with. He was potentially dangerous if he was on the wrong side. The man replied that he was not on either side, but he was the commander of the LORD's army. God did not come to Joshua as their ally, but as their leader. He did not come to join their battle, but to instruct him on how to carry out God's battle. Joshua was the leader of the Israelites, a position of some authority, but he recognized the superior authority of the One who was before him. The Israelites were only a division of God's greater army which included the angelic hosts. It was his war that the Israelites were fighting.

God had called the Israelites out of Egypt. He had led them to the Promised Land. He was the One who promised to deliver the inhabitants of Canaan into their hands. The people of the land were very wicked and God was about to punish their wickedness by using the Israelites. Therefore, it was God's battle and Joshua was just one of the participants in it. Joshua was about to be used by God to punish the inhabitants of Canaan and lead the Israelites in victory. That is why God appeared to him. He came to give him his marching orders. That is exactly what God did in chapter six. They were unusual marching orders because the battle was God's and not Joshua's.

God told Joshua to march around the city with the priests blowing trumpets. The Israelites were to march like this for six days in front of the ark. On the seventh day they were to march around the city seven times with the priests blowing trumpets. Then the people were to shout and the walls of the city would collapse. Armies do not normally win battles with trumpets, but God can use any weapons he chooses because he is God. The unusual strategy proved to the Israelites that the battle was the LORD's and not theirs. If they had won the victory through normal military means, then they might have thought that it was their own doing and not God's.

Today, the world abounds with conflicts, both major and minor. There are athletic contests, domestic disputes and civil wars. There is political tension and religious tension. Not surprisingly, many people want God to take their side in the conflict. Some people even claim that God is on their side. Muslims have been known to call their conflicts a jihad or holy war. Christians have been known to call their conflicts a crusade. In each case they claimed to be fighting for a noble, even a holy cause, and that God must be in their side in such an endeavour. Of course, the object of the crusades was to drive the Muslims out of Palestine ("the Holy Land") and often the jihads are aimed against Jews who also consider themselves the people of God and who currently occupy Palestine.

Athletes often pray before a contest. Are they praying for a victory or just praying that God will protect them from serious injury? Whose side will God take in the game, or will he take any side?

How often have you asked God to take your side? Have you prayed for your team to win the game? Have you prayed for your country to be victorious in battle? Have you prayed for your political party to win the election? If God answered your prayers, then what about the people who prayed for the other side?

Of course, the whole problem of praying for God to take our side is that it would put us in charge and that would never do. God does not take sides because God is the One in charge. As Joshua learned, God is the commander and not just one of the army. We can never ask God to take our side, but it is possible to join his side. God gave Joshua his marching orders and, if we listen, he will give us our marching orders.

Chapter 8
I Will Hear From Heaven
(2 Chronicles 7:1-22)

This passage deals with the dedication of the temple of God. During Israel's wanderings in the wilderness, they had a movable tabernacle for the worship of God. In that tabernacle they placed the Ark of the Covenant and the altars of sacrifice. When people of Israel finally came into the Promised Land, the ark, which was the symbol of the presence of God, continued to be moved about. Once it even fell into Philistine hands. David, however, brought the ark to Jerusalem, the city that he had established as the capital of Israel.

David then wanted to build a house for God to dwell in – a temple to hold the Ark of the Covenant and all the other things associated with the worship of God (1 Chronicles 28:2). God did not want him to build the temple because he was a warlike king. He chose Solomon, David's son, to build the temple (verses 5-7) Though David accepted God's will in this, he still went ahead and made elaborate preparations for its construction. He made sure that Solomon would succeed him as king by having him crowned while he was still alive (1 Kings 1:28-40). David provided many of the building materials for the temple (1 Chronicles 29:1-5). Many Israelite officials also gave generously toward the temple construction.

Soon after Solomon was established as king, God appeared to him and offered to grant him one request (2 Chronicles 1:7). Solomon asked for wisdom that he might govern the people of God well (verses 8-10). Because Solomon had been so unselfish in his request, God also promised him great wealth (verses 11, 12).

Then Solomon went ahead with the construction of the temple (2 Chronicles 2:1). He made sure that it was a magnificent building because he thought that nothing but the best was good enough for God (verses 5 and 6). This is a good example for us. Often we give God our second best, when he deserves and demands our best. When we keep the best for ourselves and give God what is second best, it shows that our priorities are wrong. It shows our selfishness.

After the temple and all its furnishings were built, Solomon had the Ark brought into the temple. Then Solomon spoke to the people and prayed before them to God. He asked God to make the temple a place where he would listen to the prayers of his people (2 Chronicles 6:12-40). Then God dedicated the temple as a place where he might be worshipped. The passage that we are studying deals with the dedication of the temple. In it we find another encounter with God and, like the other encounters that we studied, we can learn some things about God.

When Solomon had finished praying, fire came down from heaven to consume the sacrifices that he had presented to the LORD. This was a sign that God had accepted his offering. God dedicated the tabernacle in the wilderness in the same way (Leviticus 9:24). Fire was a frequent symbol of the presence of God in the Old Testament. It was also a picture of his holiness.

Also, the glory of the LORD filled the temple like a cloud. This too happened when the tabernacle in the wilderness was dedicated (Exodus 40:34, 35). God demonstrated to his people that his presence would reside in the temple in the same way that his presence dwelt in the tabernacle.

Because of their wonder at the miraculous fire that consumed the sacrifices on the altar and because of the dense cloud that enveloped the sanctuary, the priests could not enter to perform their usual duties. They were overwhelmed by the signs of the majesty of God. Martin Luther had the same experience when he performed his first mass as a monk. His hands trembled as he handled the elements. Unfortunately, this sense of awe and wonder is so often missing from our worship services. We are not often moved by awe at the signs of the presence of God in our midst as the priests were and as Martin Luther was. We have lost our sense of the majesty and holiness of God.

The immense multitude that surrounded the temple also felt the presence of God and saw the signs of his majesty and holiness. They too were overcome and fell on their faces before God. They expressed their awful dread at the divine majesty of God. They worshipped before God and showed their submission to his divine authority.

When we come into God's house to worship him, do we sense God's presence amongst us? Are our hearts filled with awe at his divine majesty and holiness? Do we come before God with reverence and submission? This is what worship is all about. This is what worship means.

When their confidence returned to them, the priests were able to approach the altar. Then they could perform their appointed duties and make the sacrifices.

They had a lot of work to do that day. Solomon's personal offering was enormous. He sacrificed 22,000 oxen and 120,000 sheep. Think of the magnitude of such an offering! Again Solomon was expressing his conviction that nothing was too good for God. As Isaac Watts put it in his great hymn: "Were the whole realm of nature mine, that were a present far too small. Love so amazing, so divine, demands my soul, my life, my all." Thus, the priests would have been very busy presenting such a sacrifice to God.

They were not the only ones that were busy that day. There were many people involved, and each had an important part in that massive worship service. The Levites worshipped God with their musical instruments. The people celebrated the goodness of God and also made sacrifices. They praised and worshipped him saying, "He is good; his love endures forever."

Solomon had to consecrate the middle of the courtyard because the altar could not contain his massive offering. He knew that worship required a sacrifice and he willingly made it. He set an example for his people. Solomon's huge offering was a peace offering, which meant that the people shared in partaking of it. Thus, the temple dedication was not only a worship service, but a great feast as well. It was a time to celebrate the goodness of God.

This celebration went on for days and when it was over, the people went away happy. Today, if a service goes much beyond an hour, many people go away grumbling. Where is that sense of worship, that joy in God's presence, that celebration of God's goodness?

God desires our worship and praise. He is pleased when we bow our hearts before him just as he was pleased when the Israelites bowed before him. He wants us to sing his praises and celebrate his goodness. We can all have a part in the worship of God. We can bring our possessions as Solomon and the people did. None of us have the kind of wealth that Solomon had, but all of us can bring the best that we have to God. We can worship God with musical instruments as the Levites did. We can proclaim God's goodness and love as the people did.

When we go to worship God, do we prepare our hearts? Do we simply sing the appropriate hymns and repeat the correct phrases without paying attention to the words? God looks past our outward actions to see our inward motivations. What does God see in us today?

After the celebration was over and the temple was dedicated to God's service, the LORD appeared to Solomon that night and spoke to him. He told Solomon that he had indeed accepted the temple as a place of sacrifice. God put his official seal of approval on Solomon's temple.

God also promised Solomon that his eyes would be open and his ears attentive to the prayers offered in the temple. He had chosen Solomon's temple for a dwelling place and promised that his name would be there as well as his heart. God not only promised that he would accept the worship and sacrifices that his people offered to him there, but he also promised that he would listen attentively to their prayers as well.

However, there were conditions attached to these promises. Verse 14, which is the best known verse in all of Chronicles, makes these conditions quite clear. Here God says that four prerequisites are necessary for a national blessing. The people of God must humble themselves, pray, seek God's face, and turn from their wicked ways before he will hear from heaven. In order for there to be a time of national blessing, there must first be a time of national repentance and prayer by the people of God. This is expressed more clearly here than in any other place in scripture. Thus, we know the steps that we must take before our nation will be blessed by God. We, the people of God, must first humble ourselves, pray, seek God's face, and turn from our sins before we have the right to ask God to bless our nation.

God promised Solomon three national blessings in return for national repentance and prayer. He promised to hear their prayers, forgive their sins, and heal their land. What more could they ask for?

God set before Solomon and the nation of Israel a clear choice. They had a choice between national judgments such as famine, pestilence and captivity, and national blessings. They had a choice between God's perpetual favour and presence with them and his abandoning them to destruction. They had a choice between life and death, between blessing and cursing. We know from history that the Israelites allowed paganism to creep in and they came to worship other gods. We also know from history that God did curse them and they were carried off into captivity.

Both the United States and Canada were founded on principles of honouring God and giving him authority. Canada is recognized as a nation under God in its constitution. Unfortunately, in many ways our nation has drifted away from God. The legalization of abortion and homosexuality have illustrated this drift, but there are other indicators as well. Empty pews in our nation's churches are a powerful indicator of Canada's drift away from the worship of God. We definitely need to turn to God as a nation.

God has set before us the prerequisites – the conditions – for a heaven sent revival. Our nation has never had a truly national revival, but the opportunity for one is available to us. The people of God in Canada need to humble themselves, pray, seek God's face, and turn from their sins. We must do this wholeheartedly because God knows our motives. God knows that some people only pray in times of distress. In fact, he mentioned that in verses 13 and 14. However, God did say that he would listen to the prayers that his people offered in such circumstances if they were offered in a true spirit of sincerity and repentance.

How sincere are our prayers? Do we truly humble ourselves before Almighty God and confess our sins? Do we truly repent and attempt to change our habits by the grace of God? Do we really seek God's face in our prayers or do we just repeat favourite phrases without meaning? Do we earnestly seek God's favour or do we merely pray out of a sense of duty? Are our prayers full of worship and praise as they should be or are they just shopping lists of things that we want from God? Do we really want God to hear from heaven and heal our land?

Chapter 9
A Still Small Voice
1 Kings (19:1-18)

In this chapter we are dealing with a very significant episode in the life of Elijah. Elijah was a prophet of God to the northern kingdom of Israel. We know surprisingly little about him and nothing about his early life. He suddenly appeared on the scene in 1 Kings 17:1, prophesying to Ahab, the king of Israel.

Ahab was a very wicked king. 1 Kings 16:30 says, "Ahab son of Omri did more evil in the eyes of the LORD than any of those before him." Ahab's biggest sin was marrying Jezebel, a Phoenician woman. It was she who led Ahab and the nation of Israel away from the worship of the true God to the worship of Baal. It was because of this idolatry that it was said of Ahab that he "did more to provoke the LORD, the God of Israel, to anger than did all the kings of Israel before him." (verse 33).

Jezebel was without a doubt one of the most evil women who ever lived. For thousands of years her name has been synonymous with immoral, vindictive meanness. Revelation 2:20 illustrates this clearly for us.

Though Jezebel tried, she could not completely stamp out the worship of the true God. The people still continued to worship the LORD even though they were now worshipping Baal. Elijah was sent by God to lead the Israelites away from the worship of idols back to the true worship of God. He set up a contest to demonstrate who was the true god. He told Ahab to gather the prophets of Baal and to meet him on Mount Carmel. Then the contest began.

The contest was a simple one. The true god would demonstrate his power by consuming the sacrifice offered to him. The prophets of Baal prepared a sacrifice, but did not set fire to the wood on the altar. They called on Baal to send fire, but no answer came. Elijah prepared a sacrifice for the LORD and had the wood soaked with water. Then he prayed and God sent fire from heaven to consume the sacrifice, and even the water dried up. Then the people declared that the LORD was the true God. The prophets of Baal were slain as false prophets.

Some time before this, Elijah had prophesied to Ahab that there would be a long drought and God fulfilled that promise. After this victory on Mount Carmel, Elijah prayed for rain and a heavy rain came.

Now there should have been a massive return to the worship of the true God, but there was not. Jezebel should have admitted defeat and confessed her sins, but she did not. She was not one to readily admit that she was wrong. When she heard that Elijah had had her prophets killed, she decided to have him killed.

Thus, Elijah was now in grave danger. He had to flee to save his life. During his flight from Jezebel, God met Elijah and equipped him to continue the battle against Baal worship. Through his experience with God, Elijah came to understand a great deal about God.

Everything was now changed for Elijah. Through his prayers, God had sent a long drought and then a heavy rain. Elijah had won the victory over the prophets of Baal, but now he was fleeing for his life. The courage that he had to face Ahab and the 450 prophets of Baal failed him when he was threatened by a woman. Elijah was afraid, lonely, discouraged and depressed. He had gone from an emotional high, when he was on top of the world, to an emotional low, when he was in the depths of despair, in a very short time. It has been speculated that Elijah had bipolar disorder – that he was manic depressive. This could be true. However, if we are honest, then we will also admit that we all have our highs and lows. We all have our good times and our bad times. Even Jesus got depressed in the garden of Gethsemane. He said to Peter, James and John in Matthew 26:38, "My soul is overwhelmed with sorrow to the point of death." To say that it is unspiritual to get depressed is only to make the depression worse. Discouragement is a normal part of life. No one can always be on top of things. We must be willing to accept defeats as well as victories. It is usually in times of defeat that God speaks to us. It is usually at such times that our greatest spiritual growth takes place. Elijah was met by God in a powerful way during his time of despair.

Elijah's mistake was in taking himself too seriously. He ran off into the wilderness and asked God that he might die. Elijah was wise to share his doubts with God because God is not fooled by our attempts at pretending that everything is all right. God did meet Elijah in his hour of need, but not by giving him what he asked for. Instead, he gave him what he needed – rest and food. Often the cause of our depression or bad mood is simply a lack of energy caused by inadequate sleep, exercise, or diet. We look for spiritual causes when the real cause is physical.

We cannot expect to win every battle in life. God never meant us to go through life untroubled. There will be times when we are on top of the mountain in victory and there will be times when we are in the depths of despair. The secret to contentment is in not taking ourselves too seriously. We must not get anxious about how we feel. We cannot go on our feelings.

Elijah's fear was real. Jezebel did mean every word of her threat against him and she did have the power to carry it out. However, Elijah should have remembered that God had considerably more power than Jezebel. Instead of bewailing his fate, Elijah should have leaned on the promises of God.

Elijah was afraid, lonely, depressed, tired, hungry and frustrated, but he found that God could meet all of those needs. He learned that God was not limited by his human weaknesses, whether they were emotional ones like loneliness and depression or physical ones like fatigue and hunger. God is not limited by our human weaknesses either. He can give us strength to meet whatever challenge is set before us. We can depend upon that.

Elijah ran as far away from Jezebel as he could go. He left Israel and went to Judah, a nation that still worshipped the LORD. However, even Judah was not far enough away. He was still afraid of Jezebel, even outside her country, so he left his servant and went into the wilderness. He ran still further away. He went to Mount Sinai. Elijah thought that the further he was from Jezebel, the safer he was. What he should have known is that God is able to protect his followers, even in the midst of danger.

Elijah thought that he was the only one who was faithful to God. Twice he said to God, "I have been very zealous for the LORD Almighty. The Israelites have rejected your covenant, broken down your altars, and put your prophets to death with the sword, and now they are trying to kill me too." (verses 10, 14) Elijah was wrong. He was not the only one left in Israel who still served God. Elijah's emotional state had clouded his reason. He should have known that God still had other servants, but he did not. God had to tell him that there were still 7,000 others in Israel who did not serve Baal. They were as visible as he was, but they still belonged to God.

One of the major causes of depression is a temporary loss of perspective. We take things too personally. We get anxious about things that are not our problem. Why should Elijah have worried about who else was serving God? Was that not God's problem rather than his? We get into trouble by trying to solve God's problems for him, or other people's problems for them, when we have enough of our own to worry about. We should instead devote ourselves to the tasks that God has given us and leave others to the work that God has given them.

Elijah learned that God was not limited by his perception of things. He had been labouring under the erroneous impression that he was the only one who was faithful to the LORD. He was frustrated because it seemed to him that the task that he was assigned was hopeless. However, Elijah only saw things from his point of view. His vision was greatly limited. God, however, saw the whole picture. He knew the whole story.

It is easy to think that tasks assigned to us are beyond our abilities. Often we feel that we are alone in life. Fortunately, God is not limited by such false perceptions. He sees things that we so readily miss. He knows what can be done. So rather than giving up like Elijah did, we should turn to God in prayer and ask for wisdom and strength to do his will.

Elijah went to Horeb, which is also known as Sinai. This is the mountain where God appeared to Moses in a burning bush. It was also where God gave the Ten Commandments. In fact, it is likely that the cave where Elijah went was the same cave that Moses hid in when God appeared to him in Exodus 33. Elijah thought that by going to the mountain where God had revealed himself, he would get closer to God. He was wrong. God does not dwell in any one special place. He is no more present on Mount Sinai than anywhere else. Twice God asked Elijah, "What are you doing here, Elijah?" He was in effect saying to Elijah, "I never sent you to this place. There is no point in coming here to seek me. I can be found anywhere." The idea of erecting shrines at places where God has manifested himself is not necessary. God is everywhere. The whole world is his shrine. Peter had to learn that lesson on the Mount of Transfiguration.

Elijah was told to go and stand on the mountain before the LORD. This is similar to God's command to Moses in Exodus 33:21. Both men experienced the presence and glory of the LORD on Mount Sinai, but there were significant differences. When God first appeared to Moses, he spoke from a burning bush. When God gave Moses the Ten Commandments, Mount Sinai was covered with smoke and the people trembled. However, when God appeared to Elijah on Mount Sinai, his presence was not manifested in the wind, the earthquake or the fire. Instead, he communicated with Elijah by a still small voice which was in vivid contrast to the tumult that preceded it. God demonstrated to Elijah that he was not limited to spectacular demonstrations of power. He is not limited to any one way of working. Sometimes he works miracles. Sometimes he does not. Sometimes he uses spectacular signs to speak to his people. Sometimes he does not. Most often he speaks by the inward voice of the Holy Spirit and his written word.

We tend to restrict the working of God to the miraculous and spectacular. We say that, if God has not spoken dramatically, then he has not spoken at all. We forget that God works in many different ways. He often speaks quietly to our hearts and minds. Perhaps he only uses the spectacular when he cannot get our attention any other way. God usually works in ways that cannot be detected.

We yearn for the exciting and the spectacular. We cry out for miracles and signs. This is what Elijah wanted. He wanted the fire from heaven to be the norm rather than the exception. Yet God taught him that his presence could be felt in stillness – in silence. When Elijah learned this, he covered his face as a sign of reverence for the presence of God. Moses too hid his face when he met God at the burning bush. We look for God in the tumult when he often manifests himself in the silence – in the stillness. Habakkuk 2:20 says, "But the LORD is in his holy temple; let all the earth be silent before him." God's presence will most often be felt in times of silence – when we quiet ourselves before him.

Elijah limited God to a specific place – Mount Sinai – and a specific way of working – the miraculous and the spectacular. God refused to acknowledge such limitations. He showed Elijah that he was present everywhere and capable of working in any way that he pleased.

Elijah was commissioned by God to appoint others to carry on the work after him. God's servants come and go, but the work of God continues from generation to generation. He is not restricted to working through any one individual or group.

We must learn that we can meet God anywhere and at any time. We also must learn not to put too much importance on ourselves. We are not God's only servants. He can and does work quite nicely without us. God works in ways that we do not expect and uses many different people to accomplish his purposes.

James 5:17, 18 says, "Elijah was a man just like us. He prayed earnestly that it would not rain and it did not rain on the land for three and a half years. Again he prayed, and the heavens gave rain, and the earth produced its crops." Elijah was an ordinary man who was used by God in a mighty way. He had the same human weaknesses that we have, but he learned that God was not limited by them. He had the same human perspective that we have, but he learned that God was not limited by that. He also had an inadequate conception of God, but God refused to be confined into the mould that Elijah had for him. These are lessons that we need to learn as well. We have a God that far exceeds the limits that we tend to set for him. He continually surprises us.

Chapter 10
Here Am I
(Isaiah 6:1-8)

Isaiah 6 is one of the best known chapters in prophetic literature. It is a passage that is loaded with significance and one that has meant a great deal to me for some time. That is why I chose it as the passage of scripture to be read at my ordination service. That was more than 25 years ago, but it is still significant to me.

This chapter describes the call of Isaiah to the office of prophet. The Bible gives the record of the calls of several prophets, but this one stands out because of its dramatic and majestic quality. It is easily the most vivid account. Here Isaiah records an experience that had a very profound and lasting effect on his life. From this moment on he was a changed man.

Verse one begins, "In the year that King Uzziah died... " For Isaiah, the timing of his call was very significant. He did not say whether he had this experience before or after Uzziah's death, but Isaiah 1:1 does say that Isaiah's prophetic ministry included some time during the reign of Uzziah. Thus, it appears that the call came before the king's death, but in the same year that he died.

Uzziah was a good and successful king. He brought an era of peace and prosperity to the nation of Judah. His death, however, marked the end of that era. From that time on, the nation began to decline and grow weak. This was also a time of international tension. Tiglath-Pilesar III had ceased the throne of Assyria and had begun a program of conquest. This growing military power posed a serious threat to the tiny nation of Judah.

Isaiah saw his nation shrink from a respected power to a vassal state during his lifetime. He was raised in prosperity, but he soon saw this prosperity come to an end. He had enjoyed peace, but he soon witnessed the ravages of war. He was called to be God's spokesman during an exceedingly difficult time, but God prepared him for that role. The most significant part of this preparation was this vision which Isaiah described for us. He told us what he saw on the day that he was commissioned as God's prophet.

Isaiah described his vision in some detail. Its effect upon him was so dramatic that he never forgot what he saw. Many commentators say that he was in the temple when he experienced this vision since his description of the vision fits in well with a temple ceremony, but this is not certain. What is certain is that Isaiah saw a vision of God enthroned in his heavenly temple. It is interesting that Isaiah describes the throne, the robe and the attendants, but not God himself. Actually, there are no descriptions of God in the Bible. He simply cannot be described. In fact, he cannot really be seen at all, as John 1:18 and 1 Timothy 6:16 point out for us. What Isaiah saw was a manifestation of God's glory, and not God himself. However, it must be pointed out that Isaiah's vision was not some kind of mystical, inward experience, but an actual vision. What he saw, he saw clearly – as clearly as he saw anything else.

Isaiah's vision was overwhelming. It was a spectacular manifestation of the presence of God himself. The door posts shaking and the smoke were both signs of God's presence. The entire scene conveys a sense of awe at the majesty of God.

The seraphs that surround the throne of God here are not described anywhere else in the Bible. They are evidently some kind of angelic beings dedicated to the praise and worship of God. The term seraph literally means "burning one". The appearance of these creatures must have been decidedly brilliant. These seraphs had six wings each. With two of them they covered their faces as a sign of reverence for God. With two they covered their feet as a sign of humility and with two they flew as sign of their constant service of God. They were continually engaged in the worship of God. They sang his praises antiphonally. They called back and forth to each other.

What the seraphs said had a tremendous impact on Isaiah. They spoke of the holiness of God. It was this concept that dominated the message of Isaiah. He frequently referred to God as "the Holy One of Israel." Holiness refers to that quality which separates God from his creation – his otherness. It is the mysterious, incalculable, unapproachable quality of God. It is his most distinguishing characteristic. The threefold repetition is the Hebrew method of expressing the superlative. What the seraphs were crying to each other is that God is most holy, he is the holiest of all. There is no one else and nothing else that can be compared with him. The seraphs also spoke of the glory of God. Glory means "heaviness, weight, power." It is the divine manifestation of God. While God is distinct from man, he still reveals himself to man and this divine revelation fills the whole Earth. There is nowhere in all of creation where God's glory cannot be seen, where his presence cannot be felt. God reveals himself to man through his creation, as Romans 1:20 says.

John 12:41 says that Isaiah saw the glory of Jesus Christ. He caught a glimpse of the pre-incarnate Son of God and this vision deeply disturbed him. It brought terror to his heart. He saw God as he was, holy and glorious. That is how we must see God. We will probably never have a vision of God like Isaiah did. Few people do. However, we do worship Isaiah's God and we do need to see him as Isaiah did, as One who is most holy and as one whose glory fills the whole earth. All too often our concept of God is inadequate. We do not see God as he really is. We need to correct that. We need to know God better. We need to search him out in his Word.

Isaiah was filled with terror when he realized that he was in the presence of God, because he realized his own unworthiness. He knew that even a conscientious, religious man like himself was not worthy to be in the presence of the holy God. Thus, he was filled with a sense of overwhelming uncleanness. His horror was not simply that of a creature before his Creator, but that of a sinful man before holy perfection. He was deeply frightened and cried out, "Woe to me! I am ruined!" Isaiah was afraid that he was doomed because he had seen God and that meant death, as Exodus 33:20 points out.

When Isaiah saw God, he also saw himself. He realized who he was. He made an honest self-appraisal and came to the conclusion that he was a sinner. Note that Isaiah's confession of sin is particular and not general. God does not want some kind of abstract acknowledgment of our general sinfulness, but an honest confession of particular guilt. Isaiah's sin was one of the lips. He realized that his tongue was difficult to tame, as James 3:8 says. His lips could not praise God because his lips were unclean. James 3:9, 10 points this truth out for us.

Isaiah knew that he had no right to be in the presence of God. He knew that, as a sinful man, he could not worship God. Before we can approach God, we must first acknowledge our sinfulness, our unworthiness, and this must be personal and particular.

When Isaiah confessed his guilt, his sin was purged. The coal that was taken from the altar was probably a heated flat stone that was used for baking. In any case, it was taken off the altar and conveyed the holiness of the altar. It illustrates the truth that true cleansing takes sacrifice. There must be a sacrifice before our sins can be forgiven. Divine mercy and forgiveness come through the altar of sacrifice.

When Isaiah's sin was purged and his iniquity was taken away, he was fit to stand in the presence of God. Psalm 24:3, 4 makes it clear to us that we need to be purified before we can approach God. Malachi 3:2 also points this out.

Isaiah had a personal experience of God's forgiveness. He knew what it was like to be cleansed of sin and guilt. We too need that personal experience. Since we must stand before God alone, we must be personally cleansed and forgiven by God. That is indeed an exhilarating experience, to feel cleansed from the uncleanness of sin. Isaiah felt that cleansing, that purifying fire. We can feel it as well if we are willing to confess our personal guilt, our particular sins.

Isaiah not only confessed his own sin to God, but his people's sin as well. He acknowledged the fact that he lived among a people of unclean lips. Note that Isaiah did not use his people's sin as an excuse for his own sin. The fact that everybody was doing it only intensified his guilt rather than relieving it. This is an example for us. We cannot excuse our sin by pointing out the sins of others.

Isaiah was a representative of his people. He acknowledged the fact that he was one with them. Even in this highly individual experience when he was personally confronted by God, Isaiah could not separate himself from his people. This is significant because, if Isaiah was to be a prophet to the people of Judah, then he could not be above them or separate from them. He must be one with them. Our Christianity is too individualistic. We tend to separate ourselves from others when we should be one with them. The Christian life can never be lived in isolation. We need to be continually in touch with others. We need to fellowship with other Christians. Without such interaction, we can never grow as Christians.

Isaiah was commissioned to be God's spokesman. He was given a message to give to the people of God. However, the message was not one of comfort and encouragement. It was instead a message of impending judgment. Note that God said to Isaiah, "Go and tell this people... " God did not refer to the people of Judah as "my people", but rather as "this people." By their conduct they had forfeited the right to be called the people of God. They were no longer good representatives of God. How do we represent God? Is he ashamed to call us his people? Do our actions glorify him?

Isaiah was called to speak to a people who would not listen to him. What a terrible task! His people would hear the word of God from his lips, but they would choose not to understand it. They would reject his message and by that rejection, harden their hearts. Distrust, disobedience and disloyalty produces moral and spiritual insensitivity. This rejection, this refusal to listen, brings down the judgment of God. Now it is natural to think that this refers to God's judgment upon sinners for their rejection of Christ, and this is true. However, this is not the whole picture. Remember that God is talking about Judah, the chosen people of God, and not some pagan nation. It is not only unbelievers who are unresponsive to God's Word. Often Christians refuse to listen to what God is saying to them. Christians can become spiritually insensitive. A Christian who is growing in Christ, who is sensitive to God's leading in his life, will continually discover things in his life that are not pleasing to God. God will point out specific areas of his life that need changing. No Christian has arrived at spiritual perfection. Therefore, if God does not appear to be speaking to you, then it is probably because you are not listening to him. If you do not come under conviction when you hear or read the Word of God, then it is likely that you have hardened your heart.

Isaiah did not separate himself from his people. He realized that he was one with them. He saw his people as there were; stubborn, unresponsive and unrepentant. Yet their hardened hearts did not alleviate his responsibility to speak to them.

Yes, this vision had a tremendous impact upon Isaiah. He saw God as he was. He saw himself as he was. He saw his people as they were. Yet the emphasis of Isaiah's record of his vision is not on what he saw, but on what God said to him. God's message of speaking to an unresponsive people was what was really important to Isaiah, and not the dramatic vision. The vision just confirmed to Isaiah that it was indeed God who was speaking to him. God's message to Isaiah was important to others as well. Verses nine and ten are referred to in all four gospels as well as being referred to twice by Paul. Isaiah was not the only one to whom the people of Israel refused to listen. Few people really listened to Christ as well.

The message that God has commissioned us to proclaim is not unlike that of Isaiah. We stress the good news of salvation and the gospel is good news to those who accept it. However, to those who reject it, God's message of salvation becomes a message of judgment. To reject God's offer of salvation is to bring judgment upon oneself. John 3:18 makes this abundantly clear. Thus, proclaiming God's message of salvation automatically means proclaiming judgment on those who reject it. This will not make us too popular, but God gives us no other message.

When Isaiah stood in the counsel of God, he heard God asking, "Whom shall I send? And who will go for us?" Isaiah responded immediately with, "Here am I. Send me!" His response is similar to others who were called by God. However, others who responded like him were personally addressed by God. Isaiah was not. God's question was worded generally, but Isaiah took it personally. God gave a commission and an opportunity to respond and Isaiah seized that opportunity. Often we expect God to call us by name, but he does not always do so. The commission to be his representative, his spokesperson, is recorded in Matthew 29:19, 20 and other places as well. We may pretend that God is not speaking to us. We may harden our hearts to the voice of God. Or we may, like Isaiah, take God's commission seriously and personally. God gives us a choice. We are not forced to be his messengers. God is asking us, "Whom shall I send, and who will go for us?" What is your response? Are you willing to say, "Here am I. Send Me?"

Chapter 11
I Am Only A Child
(Jeremiah 1:4-19)

Jeremiah was called to be a prophet in a very turbulent time. The ancient Near East was in an almost unparalleled state of turmoil. Three super powers were fighting with each other and Palestine was caught in the middle of the conflict. Jeremiah witnessed the collapse of the mighty Assyrian empire. It was Assyria who had taken the northern kingdom of Israel captive and made Judah a vassal state. Jeremiah saw the rise of the Babylonian empire and the fall of Judah to that empire. Jeremiah also experienced the constant influence of Egypt in the affairs of Judah. It was usually treaties with Egypt that got Judah in trouble. Jeremiah saw the tiny nation of Judah frequently switch allegiances between the superpowers in a futile effort to survive as a nation. The people of Judah trusted in treaties rather than in an omnipotent God. Jeremiah was called to warn them of the folly of that trust.

Jeremiah's call is recorded for us in Jeremiah 1. God said to Jeremiah in verse five, "Before I formed you in the womb I knew you, before you were born I set you apart; I appointed you as a prophet to the nations." Knew, set apart and appointed are roughly synonymous terms. These terms are used to make it clear to Jeremiah that he was God's specially chosen servant. Jeremiah was set apart for the prophetic office. He was called by God to be his mouthpiece. It is important to note that Jeremiah was called to be a prophet to the nations, and not just Judah.

Like so many others who were chosen by God for a specific task, Jeremiah was reluctant to accept that call. He was timid and felt inadequate for the task. This was in sharp contrast with the many self-appointed prophets and religious leaders of his day. Jeremiah was completely convinced that his mission was of divine origin. He really had no choice but to submit to the sovereignty of God. God assured him that he was predestined for the task and there was no mistaking God's choice.

Jeremiah's excuse was his youth and inexperience. Moses' excuse was his unimportance. Both men felt inadequate, but for different reasons.

Jeremiah felt that he could not speak with authority because he was too young. Moses felt that he could not speak with authority because he was an old failure. What both men failed to realize was that their authority came from God rather than their personality. It is supposed that Jeremiah was under 25 when he was called. The same word that is translated as child here is translated as young man in 2 Samuel 18:5.

Jeremiah was afraid that no one would listen to him because he was young and inexperienced. This was not a meaningless fear. Frequently young people are ignored just because they are young. Paul had to counsel Timothy in 1 Timothy 4:12, "Don't let anyone look down on you because you are young, but set an example for the believers in speech, in life, in love, in faith and in purity." God is not limited to speaking through older, more experienced people. Psalm 8:2 says, "From the lips of children and infants you have ordained praise because of your enemies, to silence the foe and the avenger." It is the message that is important and not the messenger. We must listen to the message of God, no matter who says it. Unfortunately, we still get caught up in the personality of the speaker instead of listening to what he is saying and in making sure that it is line with the Word of God.

Jeremiah was given a difficult task by God. It was not easy to be God's spokesman at that time. It was an awesome responsibility for a young man, but God prepared Jeremiah for his mission. Verse nine says, "Then the LORD reached out his hand and touched my mouth and said to me, 'Now, I have put my words in your mouth.'" The touching of Jeremiah's mouth was a symbolic act in a supernatural vision. It implied that God would give Jeremiah the ability to speak. Jeremiah had complained, "I do not know how to speak" (verse 6). God answered that complaint by touching his mouth. Isaiah's mouth was touched by a hot coal so that his lips might be cleansed. Jeremiah's mouth was touched by the hand of God so that his lips might be enabled to speak God's message.

The touching of the mouth symbolized the truth that the message that Jeremiah was to deliver was not his own, but God's. He was given the authority of the word of God when he complained that he lacked personal authority. Now that Jeremiah had felt the touch of the Master's hand, he was ready to begin his prophetic ministry.

Jeremiah's word was to be God's word. There was no disparity between God's Word and Jeremiah's. 2 Peter 1:20, 21 says, "Above all, you must understand that no prophecy of Scripture came about by the prophet's own interpretation. For prophecy never had its origin in the will of man, but men spoke from God as they were carried along by the Holy Spirit." This passage depicts the intimacy between God and his chosen servant. God revealed his will to Jeremiah, and Jeremiah declared it to his people.

The message that God gave to Jeremiah was not a pleasant one. It had a decidedly negative emphasis. In verse ten there are four synonyms for destruction and two for building. Jeremiah's message was to be predominately one of warning about the coming judgment of God. What was corrupt in the nation must be uprooted and torn down. Only then could God build and plant anew. This is a truth that we often neglect. We echo the words of David in Psalm 51:10, "Create in me a pure heart, O God, and renew a steadfast spirit within me," but we forget that God must first do something about the old heart. Renewal means change. Renewal means the destruction of the old ways and the old habits before new ways and new habits can take their place. This kind of change hurts. We like our old ways and habits. We have grown comfortable with them. We want renewal only if it means that we do not have to change anything, but that is impossible. Before we pray for renewal, we had better prepare for change.

We, like Jeremiah, have been called to speak for God. We may not have such a dramatic call as Jeremiah, but we have been called to God's service. All Christians are called by God. There is no escaping that truth. Also, like Jeremiah, we have been given God's message. We have the authority of the Word of God. It has been written down for us. We may try to make excuses and say that we are not gifted speakers. Neither was Moses or Jeremiah, at least in their own minds. Yet God used both of them mightily. Our authority does not come from our personality or our powerful speaking voices, but from the Word of God. Isaiah 55:11 says, "So is my word that goes out from my mouth: It will not return to me empty, but will accomplish what I desire and achieve the purpose for which I sent it." God does not say that it depends upon how forcefully the Word is proclaimed or how dynamic the speaker is. He does not say that it depends upon the age of the messenger. It is the message rather than the messenger that is important. We cannot excuse ourselves from the responsibility of delivering God's message by claiming inadequacy any more than Moses or Jeremiah could.

After God commissioned Jeremiah to be his prophet and gave him a message to proclaim, he gave him two visions. The first was a branch of an almond tree and the second was a boiling pot. Both of these visions were given to Jeremiah to confirm to him that the message he delivered would be fulfilled.

The almond tree was called the hasty tree because it was the first tree to bud in the spring. It produced flowers in January and bore fruit in March. Just as the early stirring of the almond tree heralded springtime, so the spoken word of God pointed to its rapid fulfilment. There is a play on words in the Hebrew original that is not evident in English translations. The Hebrew word for almond tree sounds like the Hebrew word for watching. This type of figure of speech is common in the Hebrew Old Testament. God told Jeremiah that he was watching to see that the message Jeremiah proclaimed would soon be fulfilled.

The second vision illustrated the impending doom that Jeremiah was to prophesy. Jeremiah saw a pot that was boiling over. This pot was facing away from the north which indicated that the disaster was coming from the north. Soon the wind from the north would overturn the boiling pot and its contents would be spilled over Judah. This is a prophetic intimation of impending disaster.

God made it plain to Jeremiah that his prophecies would be fulfilled, and fulfilled soon. What God's prophet said was as certain as if it were done. For God, word and deed are one. Psalm 33:6, 9 makes this clear to us. It says, "By the word of the LORD were the heavens made, their starry host by the breath of his mouth. ... For he spoke, and it came to be; he commanded, and it stood firm."

God promised Jeremiah that he would bring judgment upon Judah for its apostasy. The people of Judah had forsaken the worship of the true God and had begun to worship idols – things that their own hands had made. Because of this sin, God promised to bring destruction upon them. God fulfilled that promise. Judah was punished severely for its idolatry. The nation was conquered and carried off into exile, where the people learned to abhor idols and worship Yahweh alone.

When God promises judgment, we can be assured that he will fulfill that promise. The Word of God proclaims that there will be a final judgment day. On that day, those who have trusted in God and have confessed Jesus Christ as Lord and Saviour will be rewarded with the glories of heaven. However, on that day, those who have rejected Christ – those who have worshipped the work of their hands – will be punished with everlasting punishment in Hell. We can be assured that that day will come because God keeps his promises. We must warn others of the coming judgment before it is too late.

Jeremiah was naturally afraid. He knew that he would not be popular. God's spokespersons seldom are popular – especially when they are proclaiming judgment. However, Jeremiah's fear was met by a forthright command to be fearless. He was told to get ready to proclaim the message that he had been given. If he would lose courage, then God would shatter him for disobedience and lack of faith.

However, if he was faithful, then God would strengthen him for the task. The source of all spiritual victory is God, rather than man. It is he who gives us strength to carry on when all seems hopeless. God promised Jeremiah that his enemies would not overcome him. He was called of God and he could not be stopped from performing his duty. This young stripling of a prophet was made by the power of God into an impregnable city, fortified with iron pillars and surrounded with walls of brass. No one or nothing could prevail against him because God was with him.

God encouraged Jeremiah by committing a great trust to him. He was told to declare the whole counsel of God openly and plainly. He was told not to spare anyone. Everyone from the least to the greatest must hear the message. Various classes of people are mentioned. Each group opposed Jeremiah, but they could not stop him from prophesying about God's judgment. We must not spare anyone either. Everyone from the least to the greatest needs to be warned about God's coming judgment.

Jeremiah found his strength by constant communion with God. The timid young man became bolder and bolder in proclaiming God's message. He was uncompromising in his message. He pronounced impending calamity when others were predicting peace and security. Jeremiah's life was threatened. He was thrown in prison. Even still, he refused to change his message because it was the word of the LORD. The realization that he had been chosen to be the supreme mouthpiece of God to a stubborn generation drove him on relentlessly toward the fulfilment of his prophetic mission.

God promises to strengthen us as well if we are faithful in proclaiming his message, but we must refuse to compromise on the Word of God. Our message may not be popular, but it cannot be changed to suit our listeners. No matter how stubborn people are, no matter how much they refuse to listen, we must remain faithful to the Word of God. God has promised never to leave us or forsake us. We can overcome all barriers if we depend upon him for our strength.

Now we might think that Jeremiah was harsh and cruel because his message was one of judgment. However, he was not like that. He has been called the weeping prophet and the prophet of a broken heart. Jeremiah was a very emotional man. It hurt him to see his message rejected and his people and country doomed. The book of Jeremiah is unusual among the prophetic books because of the extent to which Jeremiah reveals his personal feelings in it. It is as much an autobiography as a book of prophecy. Jeremiah is revealed as a man of emotional conflict. This conflict began with his call and his reluctance to accept it. He did not want to proclaim God's message of judgment, but how could he resist the explicit call of God?

Jeremiah suffered for God. At an early stage in his ministry, he was forbidden to marry. He was frequently abused and scorned by the very people to whom he was trying to minister. He suffered intense persecution. Yet, in spite of the difficulties, God gave him strength to carry on and finish the task to which God had called him.

Jeremiah is remembered as an outstanding prophet of God, yet he thought that he was unequal to the task. He was enabled to be steadfast and loyal because he trusted in God. He overcame great opposition by depending upon God rather than his own strength. God prepared him for an exceedingly difficult task by giving him a message to proclaim, by assuring him that his message would be fulfilled, and by strengthening him. God can do the same for us if we are faithful to him. However, we must remain steadfast, loyal and uncompromising.

Chapter 12
You Want Me To Do What?
(Hosea 1:1-2:1)

In our study on encounters with God, we have looked at some very unusual encounters. Jacob wrestled with God. Abraham fed him. Moses met him in a burning bush. Elijah heard a still small voice. Isaiah had a dramatic vision. Each of these men met God in a different way. God deals differently with different people. No two encounters with God are ever the same. These men were also commanded by God to do different things. Abraham was asked to sacrifice his son, Isaac. Elijah was told to anoint some future kings and his successor. Moses was directed to lead his people out of slavery in Egypt. Isaiah was commissioned to speak to a stubborn, unresponsive people. God asks different things from different people. He equips individuals for different tasks. Because we all have different abilities and different spiritual gifts, God has different roles for us. For me to say that God must speak to you the same way that he deals with me is ridiculous. Also, for me to say that you must serve God exactly the same way that I do is equally absurd. We are different people and God deals with us differently.

In this chapter, we are looking at another man's encounter with God. Again, this encounter is unique. What is unique about this encounter is not the way God speaks with Hosea. In fact, we are not even told how God spoke to him in this passage. Whether Hosea received a vision or heard an audible voice, or God chose some other means of communication, we do not know. What makes this encounter unique is what God asked Hosea to do. That is why I have entitled this chapter "You Want Me to Do What?"

God's command to Hosea was so unusual that translators and commentators have struggled to express exactly what God meant. Let us look at a few different translations of God's command. This command is given in Hosea 1:2. The King James Version has God commanding Hosea to marry a wife of whoredoms. The New American Standard Bible tells him to take a wife of harlotry. The Revised Standard Version is very similar. All three of these translations have God commanding his prophet to marry a prostitute. Both the word whore and the word harlot mean prostitute. The New Living Translation puts it more plainly. However, it has a footnote indicating that this might refer to a promiscuous woman. The New International Version has, "Go, take to yourself an adulterous wife and children of unfaithfulness, because the land is guilty of the vilest adultery in departing from the LORD." Did God command Hosea to marry an immoral woman or a prostitute?

Commentators have had even more difficulty with this command. Some have said God would have not have issued such a command and that this passage must be interpreted allegorically. However, we must always exercise caution in interpreting any passage of the Bible allegorically. As one of my seminary professors put it, "If the common sense makes sense, I must seek no other sense." There are strong arguments that weigh against allegorical interpretation. The name of Hosea's wife, Gomer, is without significance in the story and, if the events did not actually occur, then an innocent name has been strangely maligned. There are specific details in the narrative such as the weaning of a child that argue for historicity. Also, the moral scandal which is apparently the primary reason for forcing some commentators into a non-historical view is not relieved by an allegorical view. God's command to Hosea was strange whether it is literal or figurative.

Other commentators have tried to get around the difficulty of the command in a different way. They have said that Hosea's wife was an ordinary Israelite woman at the time of her marriage and only later became a prostitute or adulterous. They view the command as written in retrospect. Some of them say chapter three comes historically before chapter one. Again, there are difficulties with such a view. The text appears to say that Hosea was commanded by God to marry an immoral woman or a prostitute and he choses Gomer. It seems that he got to pick his wife. Also, changing the details of the account to fit one's conception of what God would or would not command is problematic to say the least. Remember that God did command Abraham to sacrifice his son, Isaac.

It is quite possible that Hosea was commanded to marry a sacred prostitute. I am sure that the term, "sacred prostitute," sounds strange to your ears and some explanation of the religious and cultural background to Hosea's day is necessary. While the Israelites were commanded to worship God and God alone, Baal worship was very common. We can easily see this in Hosea 1:17 and 11:2. Baal was the Canaanite deity of rain. The Israelites came to ascribe the blessings of the land to him rather than to Yahweh. Also, union with a prostitute dedicated to the worship of Baal was thought to bring about a union of god and goddess, which would in turn release procreative power and make the land and animals of Palestine fertile. We find such practices revolting and they certainly violated God's commands, but such practices were widespread in Hosea's day.

Whether Gomer was an ordinary prostitute, a sacred prostitute or an immoral woman, we cannot be sure. The text simply does not make it clear. However, in any case, God's command is strange. Just think for a moment how you would respond if God told you to go where the prostitutes hang out and pick one for your wife. Many of God's prophets suffered persecution and hardship. Some were thrown in prison and some were put to death. However, Hosea is unique in that his suffering, in a very real sense, was his message. God's word to God's people was demonstrated in Hosea's life. His personal crisis with his wife and children illustrated God's love for his people, Israel. Only the later suffering of Jesus transcends the personal sorrow of Hosea as a medium of divine revelation.

Hosea was the first prophet to utilize the figure of marriage as a symbol for Israel's relationship with God. Few analogies depict our ideal relationship with God more graphically than that of marriage. On the other hand, no analogy more dramatically portrays the character of religious faithlessness than that of prostitution or adultery. When we read the Bible, we sometimes do not notice that the events of several years can be summarized in one verse. One such verse is Hosea 1:8. It says, "After she had weaned Lo-Ruhamah, Gomer had another son. Weaning at that time meant two or three years. Putting that same distance between the first and second child and allowing for a period of a year or two before Gomer's first born child means that Hosea's troublesome marriage lasted at least five years and probably more. Also, Hosea's children are urged to rebuke their mother in Hosea 2:2. This would mean that they have by then reached the age where they could talk. Hosea 1:1 lists several kings of Judah. Thus, we can see that Hosea's ministry was carried on over a lengthy span of years and, at least a good portion of that time was spent in what could hardly be called marital bliss.

The book of Hosea is an uncomfortable book. We do not like to deal with or even talk about adultery or prostitution. However, it has some powerful lessons to teach us. Each time we have looked at someone encountering God in the Bible, we have learned something about God.

Whatever the specific details of God's command were, Hosea was definitely obedient to it. At the command of God, he married an immoral woman. The story of the marriage is lean and spare. Of its moods, feelings, conversations and quarrels, we are not told. Nothing is said of Hosea's feelings toward the command or the process by which he implemented it. In any case, it appears that disobedience was unthinkable. We are told that Hosea's action in marrying Gomer was a portrait in miniature of Israel's relationship to Yahweh. If Gomer was a prostitute dedicated to the worship of Baal at the time of her marriage to Hosea, then the poignancy and significance of Hosea's action in taking her as his wife is all the more meaningful for understanding the relationship of Yahweh and Israel. God always remained faithful to his people, but his people kept wandering away from him. They refused to worship him and him alone and instead worshipped the gods of the nations around them.

Implicit expressions of love throb through every facet of Hosea's marital experience. Hosea loved Gomer despite her actions and he loved her with a pathos and feeling reflective to the pathos of God. God was the source of Hosea's love. He responded with love and mercy toward Gomer because he had experienced that same love in the LORD. Hosea's unreserved love and subsequent heartbreak are the mirrored reflection of a divine unconditional love and of a heartbreak that are no less real in the heart of God than in the heart of Hosea. No one before Hosea had spoken so repeatedly of God's love for his people, and no one had cast divine grace in the vocabulary of marital infidelity.

It is the profound pathos, let loose toward Israel in speech after speech, irony after irony, metaphor after metaphor, and question after question which gives the book of Hosea its fire. Time after time, Hosea summed up the sin of his people by saying that a harlot spirit had led the people astray. Harlotry may describe literal acts of illicit lust or religious acts of infidelity, abandoning the worship of Yahweh for the gods and myths of paganism. More uncompromisingly than any of his contemporary fellow prophets, Hosea condemned idolatry.

Hosea not only talked about God's love and faithfulness toward Israel, he demonstrated it in his love and faithfulness toward his wife, Gomer. Hosea not only talked about Israel's unfaithfulness toward God, he experienced it in Gomer's unfaithfulness toward him. Some have said that the fact that Gomer's second and third children are not specifically called Hosea's may be due to the fact that they might not have been his. We cannot be certain. What we can be certain of is that Gomer did become unfaithful to Hosea. Chapter two clearly says that she left him to pursue other lovers. Yet Hosea remained faithful. He still loved her.

Who would marry a prostitute? Who could love an openly unfaithful wife? Hosea could and God could. What the book of Hosea clearly teaches is that God loves the unlovable. Jesus showed this by fellowshipping with prostitutes and tax collectors. Hosea showed that by marrying an immoral woman. This is good news. We rejoice to hear that God demonstrated his love for us by sending Jesus to die for us when we were still sinners. However, there is a flip side of this good news that is not so comfortable. Hosea was commanded to marry an immoral woman. God not only loves the unlovable, he expects us to do the same. Jesus made this abundantly clearly in the Sermon on the Mount. He said in Matthew 6, "But I tell you: Love your enemies and pray for those who persecute you, that you may be sons of your Father in heaven. He causes his sun to rise on the evil and the good, and sends rain on the righteous and the unrighteous." (verses 43, 44). This is not an easy task, but it is clearly the command of God and we cannot escape it. We *must* love the unlovable if we call ourselves children of God because that is what children of God do.

There are two popular concepts of God that are refuted in Hosea. One is the concept of God as an impersonal force who simply created the universe and basically let it run itself. This concept of God makes him as being above human emotions. He never loves nor hates. However, Hosea clearly portrays God as having deep emotions. God loved the Israelites and was deeply wounded when they turned from him. He showed both compassion and anger. The other popular concept of God that is refuted in Hosea is that God is so loving that he would not punish anyone. Some who have this concept of God say that everyone will be saved. Others say that those who are condemned will not be punished eternally, but instead will be annihilated. However, Hosea makes it very clear, along with many of the other prophets, that God will indeed punish those who are disobedient. Like any responsible parent, God disciplines those he loves.

We can see God's judgment clearly portrayed in both chapter one and chapter two. The names of Gomer's children in chapter one clearly speak of God's judgment on a rebellious people. The whole point of the babies' names is to symbolize God's judgment as the explanatory clauses make clear. The name of his first child, Jezreel, spoke of God's judgment on the house of Jehu for his excessive bloodbath at Jezreel. The second child's name, Lo-Ruhamah, spoke of God no longer showing pity or compassion to the stubborn Israelites. The third child's name, Lo-Ammi, spoke of God refusing to acknowledge the Israelites as his people anymore. Although covenant terminology is not used, it is presupposed. The naming of the third child clearly signifies that God's judgment had reached a climax. This name suggested the breaking of the covenant bond of love between Yahweh and his chosen people, Israel. Remember that there was a time frame of several years of Hosea's life and prophecy involved here. The time frame may serve both to show the continuity of Hosea's family life and to hint at the forbearance of God.

In chapter two, we cannot always be certain whether Hosea was speaking about his wayward wife, Gomer, or God was speaking about his wayward people, Israel. Certainly Hosea intended to weave the two images together. Although Hosea used language similar to a divorce decree, the intent of the passage is the return of the wife and nation rather than her or its dismissal. Gomer's children were urged to encourage her to lay aside the trappings of her adulterous life and cease her adultery. These children bear the stain of her adultery because they have been contaminated by her fornication, whether or not they were illegitimate. She was to take off the apparel and jewellery which identified the prostitute, whether sacred or profane. Should Gomer fail to abandon her adulterous ways, then she would be completely rejected and humiliated. Unless she made a clean break with her adultery and its trappings, she would be stripped naked and the blessings of her present life would be removed and she would be abandoned to the wilderness which would threaten her very existence. Hosea's intention is to protect his wife from her wanton urges and protect her from further harming herself and her children. His judgment was meant to be restorative rather than punitive. Rather than demanding the life of his wife, as was his legal right, instead he reordered her life so that she might end her life of sin and come to repentance.

That is how God's judgment differs from man's judgment. It is never vindictive, but always redemptive. How often have you heard a victim's family say that the perpetrator deserved a harsher sentence? Today you hear many appeals for longer sentences so that the guilty might pay for their crimes. Their restoration is seldom mentioned. Actually, if it is mentioned at all, it is usually regarded as unlikely or even impossible. What would be our fate if God regarded our restoration as impossible?

We all need discipline. Even those of us who are older still have lessons that we need to learn, and sometimes those lessons can only be learned through discipline. We should be glad that we have a Heavenly Father who is willing to discipline us in a loving manner. Of course, God expects us to discipline in a loving manner as well. This is not easy. We must be careful to avoid a vindictive spirit and work for restoration and not punishment.

However you interpret God's command in Hosea 1:2, it sounds harsh. Whether God told him to marry an immoral woman or a prostitute, it still sounds cruel. Yet that command seems almost benign compared to God's command in Hosea 3:1. It says, "The LORD said to me, 'Go, show your love to your wife again, though she is loved by another and is an adulteress. Love her as the LORD loves the Israelites, though they turn to other gods and love the sacred raisin cakes.'" Some have taken this verse as referring to Hosea's second wife. Others have said that the events of chapter three are actually prior to the command of chapter one. The key word for sorting this controversy over the translation and interpretation of this passage is the word, "again". To whom could Hosea show love again if not his wayward wife, Gomer.

God's command to Hosea in 3:1 is, to say the least, unusual. How could God expect him to show love to a woman that had obviously rejected him. She had not only left him for another man, she had also sunk so low into sin and degradation that Hosea had to buy her back. As harsh as God's command was, Hosea did obey it. His response shows us both how costly love can be and how degraded Gomer's condition had become. He had to redeem her from her slavery to sin. The price of a slave was generally reckoned at thirty shekels of silver (Exodus 21:2; Leviticus 27:4). This, however, was not what Hosea paid to buy back his wayward wife. The varied items and measures used suggest that Hosea was hard pressed to come up with the purchase price. Normally one would resort to silver or grain in such a transaction and not both. Hosea probably did not have enough of either so he had to use both. It was at a considerable price for a poor man that Hosea had to pay to redeem his wife.

Of course, in order for Hosea to buy her back, he had to forgive her. He did impose restrictions on her behaviour, which would be expected, but he also did take her back as his wife, which would not be expected. How could Hosea forgive a woman who had so blatantly been unfaithful to him? Think of the scandal that this whole relationship had caused. The neighbours would have talked when he married a prostitute in the first place. They would have talked even more when she drifted away from him and back into a life of sin. When he bought her back, they must have been shocked and flabbergasted. How could any normal man do such a thing? Didn't Hosea have any pride or dignity? She had disgraced him and his children. He should have rejected her. Her sin was simply unforgivable.

Hosea vividly demonstrated to his wayward people that God does forgive the unforgivable. Note what Hosea 3:4, 5 says. Israel, like Gomer, after a period of deprivation, will return to the LORD and receive his blessings. God not only forgives, he restores. This should remind us of Jesus' parable of the Prodigal Son. The son came back to his father to ask for forgiveness and expected to be treated like a servant. The father ran to meet him, threw his arms around him and celebrated. He restored him to his full rights as a son. Hosea 1:10 says that the Israelites will be like the sand on the seashore and they would be called sons of the living God. This is another prophecy of restoration. Note that it is abundant restoration. There is nothing stingy or calculating about God's dealings with his people.

There are many places in scripture that talk about the abundant forgiveness of God. Isaiah 55:7 says, "Let the wicked forsake his way and the evil man his thoughts. Let him turn to the LORD, and he will have mercy on him, and to our God, for he will freely pardon." Psalm 86:15 says, "But you, O Lord, are a gracious and compassionate God, slow to anger, abounding in love and faithfulness."

God forgives the unforgivable. That is the good news. This means that, whatever sin we have committed, if we turn in sincere repentance and faith toward Christ, God will forgive us. He forgave Saul who was dragging Jesus' followers to prison and death and turned him into the great apostle Paul. He forgave Moses who murdered an Egyptian and turned him into a great leader of his people. God is abounding in love and he will freely pardon, if we confess our sins and turn from them to faith in Christ.

There is, of course, a flip side to this good news. God not only forgives the unforgivable in us, he expects us to forgive the unforgivable in others. That is what he expected of Hosea and that is what he expects of us. There are many places in scripture that teach us this truth. When Peter asked Jesus how many times he should forgive his brother, Jesus basically replied that he should not keep score. After all, love "keeps no record of wrongs" (1 Corinthians 13:5). He then related a parable of an unmerciful servant. He concluded this parable by saying in Matthew 18:35, "This is how my heavenly Father will treat each of you unless you forgive your brother from the heart." If we do not forgive others, then God will not forgive us (Matthew 6:14, 15). God demands that we forgive the unforgivable in others.

Hosea is an uncomfortable book in many ways. The idea that God would command his prophet to marry a prostitute, we find hard to believe. The fact that he would demand that Hosea buy her back when she had wandered from him and sunk into the depths of sin and degradation hits us like a hammer. We simply do not want to hear such commands from God. They make us decidedly uncomfortable. However, the book of Hosea does show us some wonderful truths. God loves the unlovable, which is good news because there is much about us that is unlovable. God disciplines us so that he might restore us. This is good news because we all need discipline and restoration. God forgives the unforgivable. This is good news because we have all said and done things that would normally be unforgivable.

However, there is a flip side to each piece of good news. The bad news is that God expects, no demands, that we follow the example of Hosea. We too must love those that are unlovable, discipline those whom we love, and forgive the unforgivable. Hosea is a tough act to follow. Jesus is even tougher, but follow him we must. Fortunately, God promises us his grace so that we can love the unlovable and forgive the unforgivable. Without the Holy Spirit working within us we could never do this, but if we surrender to him then, by God's grace, we can do the impossible.

Chapter 13
The Glory of the LORD
(Ezekiel 1:1-28)

We have dealt with the call of Jeremiah and with the call of Isaiah. In this chapter we are dealing with the call of Ezekiel. Ezekiel was a very unusual man. He has been called "a cataleptic, a neurotic, a victim of hysteria, a psychopath, and even a definite paranoid schizophrenic, as well as credited with powers of clairvoyance or levitation." This is because of the unusual behaviour that he exhibited from time to time. However, according to the book of Ezekiel, this behaviour was dictated by God.

Ezekiel was a man who was uniquely aware of God. He had several visionary experiences and the miraculous held no surprises for him. He also had a passionate zeal for God that dominated his actions. Unlike many modern men today, Ezekiel was conscious of the supernatural.

Ezekiel was a priest and the son of a priest. His father was Buzi, but we know nothing about him. Ezekiel began his life in Judah and received his training for the priesthood at the temple in Jerusalem. However, he was taken captive by the Babylonians about 597 BC, during the reign of Jehoiachin. This was the second time that Nebuchadnezzar took captives from Judah. The first was during the reign of Jehoiakim. The prophet Daniel was among these. According to Jeremiah 24:2-7, it was the best people in the land of Judah that were taken captive by Nebuchadnezzar.

Ezekiel was removed from the temple, which would have been his life, and resettled on the dusty plains of Babylon. He prophesied in Babylon near the river Kebar, which was actually an irrigation canal of the Euphrates River. His call came in the fifth year of his captivity. The latest date for his oracles was given as the twenty-seventh year of captivity. Thus, he prophesied for 22 years in Babylon. It seems that he moved about relatively freely in Babylon. He was in exile, but not a prisoner.

Verse one says that Ezekiel received his call in the thirtieth year. It seems likely that he meant the thirtieth year of his life. This was the time that he would have become a full priest had he remained at the temple in Jerusalem. It is clear that Ezekiel regarded his vision and call to be God's spokesman as coming at a crucial point in his life. Thirty was considered to be the time of full maturity. Jesus began his ministry at the age of thirty.

Ezekiel prophesied to the exiles in Babylon. He was contemporary with Jeremiah and Daniel. Jeremiah began his ministry before Ezekiel and remained in Jerusalem, prophesying to the people there. Daniel prophesied in the court of Babylon to the Gentiles who ruled over the captives. He continued his ministry long after Ezekiel.

Ezekiel was a man of great influence among the exiles. The elders frequently consulted him. He was married, but childless. His wife died about the same time as the city of Jerusalem fell to the Babylonians. The name Ezekiel means God will strengthen or God will prevail.

The book of Ezekiel is not a well known or well-understood book. It is full of strange visions and symbols. However, it is structurally simple and has an orderly framework. Ezekiel is known for his precise, detailed descriptions of things. As might be expected, the priestly element dominates his prophecies. The last nine chapters deal with a vision of the restored temple.

The book abounds in repetitions. Ezekiel wanted to make sure that his people understood his message. The phrase that is repeated most often is, "know that I am the LORD". This occurs over fifty times in the book. The basic thrust of Ezekiel's message is that God is sovereign over all and, therefore, the people should return to worshipping him, even in exile in Babylon. The message had some effect. Toward the end of the captivity, the people did put away their idols and return to following the law of God.

This first chapter of Ezekiel records his vision of God. The cloud and the fire – the most common symbols of the presence of God – made it clear to Ezekiel that he was in the presence of God. There was no mistaking the fact that Ezekiel was experiencing a revelation of God. This inaugural vision was very meaningful to Ezekiel. It revealed to him what God was like.

Ezekiel was a long way from home. He had been trained to minister before God in the temple at Jerusalem, but he was miles from there now. He knew that the God of the Israelites was God of the whole Earth, but he was used to thinking of him as dwelling in the temple at Jerusalem. Thus, when God revealed himself to Ezekiel when he was far from the temple, it had quite an effect on him. It was a great comfort to him and the rest of the exiles to know that God could appear to them by the river Kebar, amid all the sordid heathenism and idolatry of Babylonian life. They learned that God cared for them even in the punishment of their exile.

Ezekiel's vision begins with the sight of a black storm cloud. Whether this was actually in the sky at that time or whether it was part of the vision is not certain. In any case, the vision moved from the natural to the supernatural, the normal to the supranormal.

Ezekiel described what he saw in great detail, but one can easily see that he was attempting to describe the indescribable. The apostle Paul struggled with the same problem when he attempted to describe a vision that he had. He said, "He heard inexpressible things, things that man is not permitted to tell." (2 Corinthians 12:4).

Ezekiel saw four creatures forming a hollow square by being joined at the wingtips. The four corners of the square symbolized the four corners of the earth. This illustrated the fact that God is Lord over all the earth. The creatures moved quickly and incessantly. They went wherever the Spirit directed them. Their movements were sure and direct – they never turned. Also, their movements were effortless.

Beside each of these creatures was a wheel. The wheel was actually two wheels bisecting each other at right angles so that it could move in any direction without being turned. The wheels moved with the creatures. In fact, when the creatures left the ground, so did the wheels. The wheels and the creatures formed part of a chariot. This chariot was infinitely mobile and was not at all earthbound. It could easily lift itself into the air. The image that is presented is one of effortless mobility.

By appearing to Ezekiel in far-off Babylon and by coming on an extremely mobile chariot, God revealed to Ezekiel that he can manifest himself anywhere. In fact, he is everywhere at once. There is no place where he cannot reveal himself. There is no place outside of his realm. He can manifest his presence even in the midst of pagan idolatry.

Ezekiel learned that God was by no means limited to the temple at Jerusalem. He knew this before, but now he experienced that as a reality. From now on, he would never doubt that God was with him and that God cared for him even in this strange land.

We too can experience God's presence and comfort no matter where we are. Whether we are laid up on a hospital bed, or whether we are miles from home, or whether we are on an open field as Ezekiel was is not important. God is not restricted to any one place. He can reveal himself anywhere. This is a great comfort to us just as it was a great comfort to Ezekiel.

Each of the four creatures had four faces. The creatures were arranged in a symmetrical pattern such that, no matter which way one looked, you could see all four faces – a different face on each creature. The four faces represented the four highest forms of life on Earth. Man is supreme over creation. The lion is the chief of the wild beasts. The ox is the chief of the domestic animals. The eagle is chief among birds. The face of the man symbolized intelligence; the lion, majesty and boldness; the ox, strength and patience; and the eagle, swiftness and piercing sight.

The noise of the movement of the creatures wings was like that of an army on the move. This illustrated the omnipotence of God. He is often called the LORD of hosts which means LORD of the armies. That his voice could be heard above the tumult illustrated his command over the chariot.

In the center of the vision was the throne. The throne symbolized sovereignty, triumph, judgment and government. God was in total control of the chariot throne. He was enthroned in the centre of the vision to show that he had sovereignty over all of creation.

God came to Ezekiel in the midst of a storm to demonstrate that he was in total control of nature. He had power over the wind, the cloud, the fire and thunder, which were all part of the vision. God came in the midst of the storm to show that he came to judge his people for their sinfulness – their idolatry. However, there was a calm after the storm to illustrate the truth that God's mercy came with his judgment. This was graphically symbolized by the rainbow – the sign of God's covenant with Noah after the flood.

God powerfully demonstrated to Ezekiel that he is sovereign over the whole Earth – over all creation. His power was not limited to Judah, but he was Lord over Babylon as well. He demonstrated this by appearing on his throne in Babylon. Ezekiel may have thought that God had forgotten his people or that God would not intervene in his situation, but that was not true. God did intervene to demonstrate his power in Ezekiel's situation.

We may think that the situation that we are in is outside God's jurisdiction. We may feel that God cannot or will not help us, but that is not true. No situation is beyond his control. He is Lord over all. He has healed the sick and raised the dead. He has brought entire nations down to destruction. Even those who do not believe in him are used by him to work out his purposes. He can do anything. We can turn to him to help us in whatever difficulties that we face. He is only a prayer away. He sits on his chariot throne waiting to speed to our aid.

Ezekiel approached God with extreme caution. He first focused his attention on the features of the vision that were furthest from God, and only later did his eyes move to the throne. Ezekiel showed a reverence, a holy fear in the presence of God. As Ezekiel was of priestly descent, it was inevitable that the aspect of God which he felt most deeply was his holiness.

The vision of the LORD riding upon his chariot throne typifies this sense of otherness and majesty that captivated God's prophets. It was utterly splendid, mysteriously intricate, superhuman and supernatural, all-seeing and all-knowing. It demonstrated to Ezekiel that God is separate from his creation. Everything connected with God derives holiness from him. It becomes set apart for his peculiar purpose.

Although the creatures were not actively involved in the worship of God, they were still affected by his presence. They did not have to cover their eyes because they were looking away from God and not at him. However, the holiness of his presence did make it necessary for them to cover their bodies with their wings.

Ezekiel struggled to describe what he saw. Note his hesitancy in his choice of words. He knew that God could not be visibly expressed and that is why making images of him is forbidden. However, God did condescend to reveal himself to man from time to time. The only form that man could conceive of God was in terms of himself, so God usually appeared in a form like that of a man, as was the case here.

When Ezekiel's eyes fell upon the manifestation of God, he fell facedown. This was a reaction similar to John's when he saw the vision that is recorded for us in the first chapter of Revelation. Ezekiel was filled with awe and reverence in the presence of the majesty of God. Throughout his ministry he carried with him that sense of holy fear that is the mark of a true prophet of God. The more one comes to know God, the more one comes to feel awe and reverence. No one can take a familiar attitude toward God. He is too majestic and holy for that. He can never be approached casually or spoken of lightly. He will not allow that.

Ezekiel came from the presence of God indelibly marked with the glory of God. There is a reverence – a radiance that marks one who has been in the presence of God. When Moses met with God, his face shone. The glory of God cannot leave us unaffected. God's holiness is contagious.

Ezekiel had been raised to serve God as a priest. The worship and service of God was nothing strange to him. He learned a great deal about God in his priestly training. However, when God revealed himself to Ezekiel by a personal encounter, everything changed. Before this, Ezekiel had a theoretical knowledge about God. Now he had an experiential knowledge. God was no longer just an abstract idea to him, but a present reality. He learned a lot about God before, but now he knew God. This made all the difference in his life. He had been *taught* that God was everywhere, but now he *knew* that because he had personally encountered him. Before he had been *taught* that God was the ruler of the whole earth, but now he *knew* that because he had seen him enthroned in pagan Babylon. Before he had been *taught* that God was holy, but know he *knew* that because he had felt his presence and had fallen on his face before him.

Each of us must personally encounter God. Second-hand knowledge about him is not good enough. We must personally experience his reality in our lives. God is ready to reveal himself to us if we ask him to do so.

Isaiah 55:6 says, "Seek the LORD while he may be found; call on him while he is near." You can meet him today if you open your heart to him. You will have a whole new outlook on life. You cannot meet God without being changed by him.

Chapter 14
A Barren Woman
(Luke 1:5-7, 39-45, 57-60)

In this chapter we are looking at a very unusual encounter with God. Elizabeth encountered the baby Jesus while he was still in Mary's womb. We can imagine encountering God in a vision or in a burning bush. We can visualize the incarnate God walking on water, feeding the multitudes and raising the dead. However, how many of us have ever thought much about God being in Mary's womb? Can you contemplate the Creator of the universe as a fetus? How could the omnipotent God be in such a helpless and dependent form?

Luke's account of the events surrounding the birth of Jesus is a very interesting one. He is the only one who wrote about of the origin of the John the Baptist and he described some events surrounding the birth of Christ that the other gospel writers failed to mention. It is interesting to compare his narratives about the birth of John the Baptist and the birth of Jesus. In both cases the announcement was made by the angel Gabriel. In both cases the circumstances of the birth and the circumcision are described. In both cases this was followed by a prophetic utterance. Luke brought out the wonder of the Messianic age. Prophecy had ceased at the close of the Old Testament. Now, in this new age, the prophetic gift was renewed.

In this chapter we encounter Elizabeth and Zechariah as well as Mary and others. Sometimes Luke's focus was on Zechariah and sometimes it was on Mary. Elizabeth appeared to have a subordinate role in the drama that unfolded. However, her role was far from insignificant. One of the first things that we find out about her is that she was barren. This is an important fact that we must not miss. Jewish rabbis said that seven people were excommunicated from God and the list began, "a Jew who has no wife, or a Jew who has a wife and who has no child." They thought that being childless meant that one was cursed by God. Childlessness was a valid ground for divorce. Zechariah could have divorced Elizabeth, but he chose to remain married to her.

Why did Zechariah refuse to divorce Elizabeth? It would appear that, except for her barrenness, she was a good wife. What did he see in her? What made her a good wife?

Zechariah was a priest, which means that he was a descendant of Aaron, the brother of Moses. Priests were permitted to marry only women of absolutely pure Jewish lineage. They were not even allowed to marry widows, only virgins. It was considered especially meritorious to marry a woman who was also a descendant of Aaron. Thus, we can see that Zechariah's marriage to Elizabeth would have pleased those around him until they came to realize that she was barren. Since they considered barrenness to be a curse from God, they might have wondered what Elizabeth had done to deserve her fate.

However, the first thing that Luke tells us about Elizabeth is that she was upright in the sight of God. This, of course, meant that she had served God faithfully, not that she was sinless. While Luke does mention that she kept the law, uprightness means more than that. It means an honourable testimony of piety towards God. It means that no fault or deficiency could be found in her. She had a real love for God and a sincere regard for his laws. Elizabeth kept the rites and customs that God had ordained or appointed. She performed all of the duties of her religion that were known to her.

Elizabeth and Zechariah were not unequally yoked. They were both of the same mind and persuasion. They were both devout and faithful. Here we have a picture of the noblest form of Old Testament education, an example of a couple who were both committed to serving God as best as they knew how. This made their childless state hard to understand since the people of that day held that God would bless his faithful servants by giving them children. Their childless state continued for some time. Luke mentioned that they were both well along in years. Thus, there was no reason to think that they would ever have any children. They could expect no change in their situation. Zechariah could have been very old at this time since there was no retirement age for priests.

They did want children. Some couples today decide for various reasons to remain childless, but Zechariah and Elizabeth had prayed for children. We know that because the angel Gabriel mentioned to Zechariah that his prayer had been heard. However, God did not answer their prayers, at least not right away. That Zechariah and Elizabeth remained upright and devout for so many years without being blessed by God with children shows the integrity of their faith. They served God out of true devotion rather than for selfish reasons.

The same angel Gabriel that told Zechariah that he was going to have a son also went to Mary with good news. He told her that she too would have a special son even though she was a virgin. We hear of two impossible births announced by the same angel in the same chapter of Luke. Gabriel also told Mary that her relative Elizabeth was pregnant. Mary got ready and hurried off to see her. She must have left soon after Gabriel's visit. When she got there, her first glance at Elizabeth would have confirmed the truth of what Gabriel had told her. At six months, Elizabeth was obviously pregnant. She had remained in seclusion until she began to show, but now she was ready to face the public with the good news.

We do not know how close a relative Elizabeth was to Mary. Cousin is an inaccurate translation. However, we do know that the two mothers had a bond of sympathy. When they greeted each other, they both burst into song. Luke tells us that Elizabeth's baby leaped in her womb when Mary greeted her. This is a common instance with unborn babies of that age. However, Elizabeth was filled with the Holy Spirit to understand what had happened to Mary. She understood the baby's leap to be an expression of joy. This leap, together with the guidance of the Holy Spirit, enabled Elizabeth to recognize Mary for what she was. She obviously knew Mary before, but she did not know that she had been especially favoured by God. She spoke in a loud voice. Her excitement showed. "Blessed are you," is the Hebraic equivalent of the superlative. It might be better translated as, "You are the most blessed of women."

Although our Bibles have Elizabeth's words in prose, they are actually poetry, just like Mary's song, which has been called the Magnificat, and Zechariah's song, which has been called Benedictus. All three spoke praise to God under the power of the Holy Spirit. These three are the first New Testament hymns and they are very beautiful.

Elizabeth's use of the title, "my Lord," indicates that she knew that Mary's child would be the Messiah. She assured Mary that what Gabriel had promised would surely take place. She encouraged her to have faith in his prophecy. We should not miss the absence of jealousy in Elizabeth's attitude towards Mary. It would be normal for an older woman who had been the recipient of such a special blessing from God to try to guard her position jealously. Some women might have commented on the fact that she was the devout wife of a priest and had miraculously conceived a child in her old age. On the other hand, Mary was a young woman who was pregnant out of wedlock. However, Elizabeth knew by faith that Mary had been uniquely favoured. In genuine humility, Elizabeth recognized that Mary had received a superior blessing.

If we are honest, then we will admit that pride is a problem for every one of us. The worst kind of pride is spiritual pride. There is a strong temptation to think that you are somebody special when you have been blessed by God. Elizabeth, however, did not succumb to that temptation. She maintained her humility even though God had miraculously intervened into her life. We need more men and women like Elizabeth. We need more humble people who are willing to let others get the special attention and honour. Someone once said that it would be amazing how much could be done for God if no one was concerned who got the credit, and he was right. Elizabeth was quite willing to admit that Mary was more favoured by God. Her son, John the Baptist, had the same attitude. He dropped back into the background so that Jesus could have the limelight.

In Palestine, the birth of a boy was an occasion of great joy. When the time of the birth was near at hand, friends and local musicians gathered near the house. When the birth was announced and it was a boy, the musicians broke into music and song and there was universal congratulations and rejoicing. If it was a girl, then the musicians went silently and regretfully away. So in Elizabeth's house there was double joy. At last she had a child, and the child was a son.

Since Zechariah and Elizabeth were so old and previously childless, the birth was clearly of widespread interest among the mother's family and friends, and many of them came to share her joy. Many of them must have hung around for some time, since they were still there when it was time to circumcise the boy on the eighth day. This was the time when boys were named. Girls could be named any time within thirty days of their birth. It is curious that the relatives tried to name the child. This was the prerogative of the parents. When Elizabeth insisted that he would be called John, they tried to enlist the help of his father, Zechariah, who declared that his name was John. Both he and Elizabeth heeded what Gabriel had told him and named their son exactly as they were instructed.

In Palestine, names were descriptive. Sometimes they described a circumstance attending the birth of the child such as Esau and Jacob. Sometimes they described the child. Laban means white or blond. Sometimes the child received a parental name. Often the name of the child described the parent's joy. Samuel means asked for. Sometimes the name was an expression of the parent's faith. Elijah means Yahweh is my God. This was significant at the time since Baal worship was predominant. Elizabeth's relatives were surprised when she said that her son was to be called John. It means Yahweh's gift or God is gracious. It was a name which God had ordered to be given to the child and it described the parents' gratitude for an unexpected joy.

A question of the neighbours and all who heard this amazing story was, "What will this child turn out to be?" His birth had been miraculous and Zechariah could speak again. The announcement of the angel and all of the circumstances of his birth and naming made it clear to everyone that this was indeed a special child. When Zechariah burst into song, he said that his son would be a prophet and would prepare the way for the Lord. Gabriel had promised that he would be great in the sight of the Lord and that his birth would be a cause of great celebration for many. This came true.

Elizabeth was blessed by God. She who was barren miraculously conceived a child in her old age. She had a son who turned out to be the greatest prophet before the coming of Christ. He was the one who turned the people of Israel back to God and prepared them for the coming of the Messiah. She was a simple country person who was specially favoured by God. We do not know why she was chosen for her role, but that does not matter. God has his own reason for choosing people.

Elizabeth was upright. She served God with devotion and kept his laws faithfully. She was also humble. Even though she had been specially blessed by God, she recognized that her relative, Mary, was uniquely favoured. She refused to be jealous when God honoured someone more than her.

Chapter 15
A Righteous Man
(Matthew 1:18-25)

God revealed himself to various people in many different ways. As Hebrews 1:1 puts it, "In the past God spoke to our forefathers through the prophets at many times and in various ways." Last chapter, we began looking at people who encountered God in a very surprising way. They encountered God as a tiny, baby boy. They came face to face with the incarnate Jesus Christ. As Hebrews 1:2 continues, "but in these last days he has spoken to us by his Son, whom he appointed heir of all things, and through whom he made the universe." The first man to encounter the baby Jesus was Joseph, the man whom God appointed as his earthly father. We know little about Joseph. Most of what we do know about him is contained in this short passage of scripture in Matthew. While this passage begins with, "This is how the birth of Jesus Christ came about," it actually focuses on the experiences of Joseph. Luke told the story of the birth of Jesus from the viewpoint of Mary, but Matthew related it from Joseph's perspective. Even the miraculous conception of Jesus was related only as its discovery affected Joseph. Matthew explained that Joseph is the legal father of Jesus in the royal line of David, but not his actual father in the biological sense.

In order to properly understand this passage, we must understand the Jewish laws and customs that existed at that time. There were three stages of marriage under Jewish law. The first was the engagement. It was often arranged by the parents, perhaps with the help of a matchmaker, when the couple were still children. Frequently, the couple had not even actually seen each other. Obviously, no courtship as we know it was involved. Engagement was not legally binding. It could be broken if the couple was not willing to go through with the marriage. However, if they were willing, then it was ratified by a betrothal. This betrothal normally lasted about one year and was binding. It was more like a legal contract than what we call an engagement. It could only be terminated by death which left the betrothed a "widow" or by a divorce as if it was a full marriage. Joseph and Mary were betrothed. He was considered to be, in a sense, already her husband, and was called such in verse 19. However, Mary remained in her father's house. This was the second stage of the marriage process. The third stage was the marriage proper. The husband took his betrothed to his home in a public ceremony and normal marital relations began. At this time, Joseph had not yet done that.

How long Joseph and Mary had been betrothed we do not know, but it must have been a few months, long enough for Joseph to discover that Mary was pregnant. It is evident that Mary had not told him about her encounter with the angel, Gabriel. We are not told why she had not confided in him. It is likely that she thought that he would not believe her. Of course, sooner or later, the discovery of her pregnancy would have been inevitable. It is this discovery that shocked Joseph. He knew that the child was not his and he would have considered Mary to have been unfaithful to him. Mary was innocent, but Joseph was not yet satisfied of her innocence. He did not yet know that the Holy Spirit was responsible for her pregnancy and not any man.

Jesus had no human father. However, every boy needs a father and mother. God had ordained Joseph for that role. Raising a divine child was obviously not an easy task. Joseph had to be a special person. Why did God choose him for this role?

Infidelity during betrothal was considered adultery and adultery was a serious crime. In Egypt, it was punishable by cutting off the nose of the adulteress. In Persia, the nose and ears were cut off. In Judea, the punishment was death by stoning (Leviticus 20:10; Exodus 16:38; John 8:5). This punishment was mandated even if the couple were not actually married, but betrothed (Deuteronomy 22:23, 24). A breach of faithfulness on the part of the betrothed was treated as adultery. Thus, Joseph had the legal right to have Mary stoned. He could have subjected her to a painful and ignominious death. Had Mary been connected to a cruel, passionate and violent man, then she would have died in disgrace. However, God had ordered it so that she was connected to a mild, amiable and tender man.

While in Old Testament times, the penalty for infidelity was stoning, by the time of Jesus, divorce was the rule. That is what Joseph was considering when he found out that Mary was pregnant. The Law of Moses definitely gave him that right (Deuteronomy 24:1). Since he thought that Mary had betrayed him, it was only natural that he would have thought that taking her as his wife would have been foolish, if not wrong. One is obliged to respect and sympathize with his motives as he evidently loved Mary and was appalled to find her untrue to him as he supposed. It was customary in a bill of divorce to specify the reasons for the divorce and to have witnesses present. However, it was permissible to limit the witnesses to two and make the divorce as quiet as possible. Joseph could give Mary a bill of divorcement without a public trial.

Joseph did not want Mary to go through the shame of a public divorce. He did not want to make a public spectacle of her. As a good Jew, he could have shown his zeal by branding her with public disgrace, but he was not that kind of man. Joseph did not want Mary exposed to scandal. It was not his purpose to make a public example of her.

When we think about it, we can easily see that this was indeed a trying time for both Mary and Joseph. Joseph must have loved Mary, but his character was likely to be ruined and he deemed it proper to be separated from her. Think of the gossip that must have flowed around in the small town of Nazareth.

Thus, we know that Joseph was a kind and tender hearted man. He was unwilling to hurt his betrothed wife, Mary, any more than was absolutely necessary. Since Joseph was a kind man he had a short but tragic struggle between his love for Mary and his legal conscience. Note that he did not act hastily, but considered carefully what he should do. In this struggle he was given divine aid. Surely, Joseph needed God's help in his dilemma if ever a man did. Joseph was a kind and gentle man faced with a very difficult decision and he needed God's guidance.

All too often, people who claim to be Christians are harsh and judgemental. They treat those who are not as "righteous" with contempt. They respond with "righteous indignation" when they feel that they have been ill treated. How kind and gentle are you? Do you insist on your legal rights? Do you want those who have hurt you punished and humiliated? Pray for God's grace so that you can be more like Joseph. Pray that you might have that same kind of spirit that he had. Pray that love and gentleness would rule your heart rather than vindictiveness and hatred.

While Joseph was pondering what to do about Mary's evident unfaithfulness to him, he had a dream. Dreams were common methods of divine revelation in Old Testament times. We do not know how people knew the difference between a regular human dream and a divine revelation, but somehow they did, or at least Joseph did. God did speak to him, or at least an angel did. The word angel literally means messenger. God sent a message to Joseph in a dream. He does guide those who earnestly seek him. Joseph had pondered and planned as best as he knew. Now God called a halt to his plans and set a different course of action for him.

The angel addressed him as "Joseph, son of David". "Son of" in the Bible often means descendant, as it does here. Even though Joseph was only a poor carpenter he was in the royal line of David. It was prophesied that the Messiah would come from that royal line. As the son of David, it was necessary for Joseph to take Mary to his house to establish Jesus' legal

Davidic lineage. If Joseph had not taken Mary as his legal wife, then Jesus could not have claimed royal descent. Thus, we can see the guidance of Joseph's movements by divine revelation and God's direction of Jesus' birth, which was the focus of Matthew's thought.

The angel told Joseph, "do not be afraid to take Mary as your wife" (Matthew 1:20). Do not hesitate to carry out your original plans and marry her. Have no doubts about her virtue and piety. Do not be afraid that she will be unworthy of you or disgrace you. You thought that she had betrayed both you and God. Instead she has been especially favoured by God. She has not been unfaithful to you at all. Her child is not the product of some illicit union, but the miraculous conception of the Holy Spirit. That Jesus was conceived by a virgin mother without the agency of Joseph or any other man is clearly stated throughout this section. The doctrine of the virgin birth of Jesus Christ is very important. It is one indication of the fact that Jesus was both the Son of Man and the Son of God.

The angel told Joseph to name the son that Mary would bear, Jesus. Names in the Bible, especially divinely revealed names, are full of meaning. Jesus is the Greek form of the Hebrew Joshua and it means Yahweh is salvation. Jesus came to Earth to bring salvation to his people. He came to deliver us from our sins. He came to pay the ransom for us. Matthew also quotes Isaiah 7:14 and says that Jesus' birth was a fulfilment of the prophecy. There Jesus was given the name Immanuel. Immanuel means God with us. This name reminds us that God came down to earth to live amongst us. We cannot say that God does not understand us. He became one of us in order that he might both understand us and redeem us.

While the virgin birth of Jesus is clearly stated in both Matthew and Luke, it is unprecedented in all history. In fact, of course, it is humanly impossible. How many of us would believe it if some woman told us that she was going to have a baby, even though she was a virgin? I bet that it would take more than a dream to convince most of us. However, Joseph did believe what the angel had told him. Joseph was not only a kind and gentle man, he was a man of faith. It took great faith to raise the Messiah, and Joseph had that faith.

Joseph had decided not to stone Mary as he could have under the law. He also decided not to expose her to the disgrace and shame of a public divorce. Now he was faced with another decision. He had to decide whether he was willing to do as the angel said and shelter Mary by marrying her. He had to decide whether to take upon himself the shame of an out of wedlock child.

Joseph wasted no time in deciding what to do. Verse 24 says that when he woke up he did what the angel had commanded and took Mary home as his wife. The marriage was formally completed, but not consummated before the birth of Jesus. Thus, Jesus was given the name of Joseph and the legal lineage of David.

One can only imagine the relief and joy of Mary when Joseph decided to marry her. He could have had her stoned. He could have publicly shamed and divorced her. He could have divorced her quietly, as he intended to do. She could have been forced to raise a child on her own with all the stigma and difficulty that would have been attached to that task in that day. Instead, she had a husband to take away her shame and embarrassment. She had a father for her child. She had a place in society.

While verse 25 says that Joseph had no union with her until the birth of Jesus, it certainly does not say that he never had any union with her. Jesus' brothers who are mentioned in the gospels were subsequently born in the normal way. There is no biblical warrant whatsoever for the 'perpetual virginity' of Mary.

Joseph was a man of action. He did what the angel had commanded him to do as soon as it was possible to obey. He took upon himself an incredible responsibility in response to a divine dream. This was not just a one time decision. Its implications lasted for years. Joseph raised a child that was not his own. We do not know what it meant to raise the Messiah, the Son of God, but it must not have been easy. We do know that Joseph was poor, but he raised several good children. James and Jude, the authors of two of the books of the Bible, were Joseph's sons. We do not know how long Joseph lived, but we do know that he was still alive when Jesus was twelve.

Joseph not only believed what the angel had said to him, he acted on that belief. That is the difference between mere belief and real faith. Real faith acts. Are you willing to step out in faith as Joseph did? Are you willing to risk shame and embarrassment for Jesus?

Joseph showed that he was an upright man in a difficult situation. He showed that he was a kind man by refusing to have Mary stoned or publicly divorcing her when he thought that she had been unfaithful to him. He showed that he was a man of faith when he took the angel at his word when what he said was humanly impossible and unprecedented. He showed that he was a man of action when he took Mary as his wife as soon as he woke up from his dream. We need more men and women like Joseph. We need Christians who are kind and considerate rather than harsh and judgmental. We need Christians who have faith in God. We need Christians who are willing to act on their beliefs. Are you willing to be like Joseph? Are you willing to show kindness and put your faith into action?

Chapter 16
The Common Man
(Luke 2:8-20)

Often, when we think about the story of the birth of Jesus Christ, we focus on the supernatural. We emphasize the virgin birth, the announcement of the angels and star that guided the magi. Even our pictures of the nativity often have a halo around Jesus' or Mary's head. This is unfortunate. There is much about the birth of Jesus that is not spectacular and miraculous. Actually, it was the conception of Jesus that was supernatural. That Jesus was conceived by a virgin is, of course, humanly impossible. It was a miracle. However, there is nothing in the gospel records to indicate that Jesus' actual birth was anything other than normal and natural.

Although Jesus' birth was heralded by angels and he was visited by shepherds and magi, there is much about his birth that was humble and ordinary. He was not born in a palace or a fancy hospital. In fact, he was laid in a manger, a feeding trough for cattle. His parents were not rich or influential, but poor, ordinary people. It is important that we remember this. Although Jesus was God himself, incarnate, the King of kings and Lord of lords, he came to Earth for the common man, ordinary people like you and me.

I want to focus on that very fact, that Jesus came to Earth to redeem the common man. Last chapter we dealt with Joseph, the legal father of Jesus. Joseph was a poor carpenter, a humble tradesman.

This chapter, I want to focus on the shepherds that came to see the baby Jesus. It is fitting and wonderful that the first announcement of the birth of the Messiah would be to humble shepherds. It is to simple men of the fields that God's message of salvation first came. Shepherds were despised by the orthodox Jews of Jesus' day because the demands of their job made it impossible for them to observe all of the meticulous rules and regulations of the ceremonial law. They were considered unreliable and were not allowed to give testimony in law courts. They had a reputation for dishonesty. There is no reason for thinking that these particular shepherds were anything other than devout. Why else would God have granted them the privilege of witnessing the birth of his child? However, they did come from a despised class.

These shepherds may have been the ones in charge of the temple flock. The animals that were sacrificed in the temple had to be without a blemish. Also, many people travelled a great distance to worship at the temple. It was not always possible to bring an animal with them. Therefore, a special herd of sheep was kept near Bethlehem. Flocks were normally supposed to be kept in the wilderness. A rabbinic law stated that any animal found between Jerusalem and a spot near Bethlehem must be presumed to be a sacrificial victim. However, even if these shepherds were the ones in charge of the temple flock, they would still have been despised by many pious Jews.

This story is brief. We do not know much about these particular shepherds. However, we can glean a few facts. We can gain an idea of what type of people they were. The angel who appeared to the shepherds is not identified. It is evident that his appearance struck terror in their hearts as the splendour of the Lord blazed around them. This was a very common reaction to a manifestation of God's glory. The angel first reassured them and then went on to explain that he had come with good and joyful news. The term gospel means good news. Thus, these humble shepherds were the first to hear the gospel.

The people normally means the people of Israel. The news of the Saviour would mean much to people in every land, but it first came to the ancient people of God. Note that the angel said that the good news is for all the people. The message of salvation was never meant just for the elite, but for the common man. That is why it is fitting that it first came to a group of despised men.

Luke recorded what these shepherds were doing when the angel appeared to them. They were living out in the fields near Bethlehem, watching over their sheep. They were out under the open sky. This was commonly done in that day. To keep their flock from straying, they spent the night with them. They were out at night, which would mean that the weather was mild. This would seem to indicate that the traditional date for Christmas is inaccurate, but we cannot be certain. Note that it was in these very pastures that David fought the lion and the bear to protect his sheep. The plural here probably means that they watched by turns. They took turns watching over the flock throughout the night watches.

Watching sheep at night is not glamorous work. If nothing happens, then the job is boring. If something does happen, then the job is dangerous. There are a lot of jobs like that. Security guard is one of them. Firefighter is another. You can go through a whole day with nothing happening. There would be a strong temptation to doze off or at least let your mind wander. Of course, these shepherds could not afford to do that. They would never know when a lion or bear would show up or a sheep would wander off. It was very important that they would be vigilant in their task. These shepherds had to be faithful. God requires that of all of us, no matter whether our jobs are prestigious or not, whether they are dangerous or not. There are many admonitions to be watchful and faithful in the Bible. These shepherds were watchful and faithful and they were alert to one of the greatest sights that people have ever seen. They saw the angel and they saw the baby Jesus because they were watchful and faithful.

The angel announced that a saviour had been born and that Saviour was "Christ the Lord". This expression is used nowhere else in the New Testament. Perhaps we should understand it as Christ and Lord. Christ is Greek for Anointed One. Anointing was for special purposes like that of a priest or king. The Jews were waiting for a special deliverer who would not simply be an anointed one, but the anointed one, the Messiah. It is this one that the angel announced. Lord is often used in the Septuagint for Yahweh or God. Thus, Christ the Lord describes the child in the highest terms possible. These faithful shepherds were invited to witness an event unparalleled in human history.

The angel completed his message by giving the shepherds a sign. This sign would not only help them recognize the baby, but it would attest to the truth of the angel's words. In Bethlehem that night there might have been one or two babies wrapped in strips of cloth, that would be common enough. However, there would have been only one baby lying in a manger.

Verse 13 says, "Suddenly a great company of the heavenly host appeared with the angel... " The word translated host is a military term for a band of soldiers. It is interesting that an army came to announce peace. They first spoke of the glory of God which is a necessary prerequisite for peace on earth. Peace, of course, means peace between men and God, the healing of the estrangement brought about by man's wickedness. True peace exists only among those who are subjects of God's goodwill and who are characterized by goodwill toward men and God.

The shepherds appear to have been pious men. They were waiting for the coming of the Messiah. They must have been shocked when his birth was announced to humble men like them. They were certainly frightened when the angel first appeared to them. However, while it is one thing to hear good news, it is another to respond to it.

When they heard the voice, the shepherds all agreed that they should go and see for themselves what had happened. It is difficult to convey in English the sense of urgency that the Greek has, but one try is, "Come on, let us go." On the first intimation that the Messiah had actually appeared, the shepherds went with haste to find him. We are not told whether they abandoned their sheep or left a few of their number in charge of them. Certainly they could have trusted God to take care of them on such a special night. We are also not told exactly how far they had to travel reach Bethlehem, only that it was nearby.

It would be great if everyone's response to the good news of salvation was so immediate. The shepherds must have been satisfied that what the angel had said to them was true, or they would not have gone to Bethlehem. It was incredible news, but they believed it anyway. Not everyone responds the same way. Some will not believe that salvation is offered to them as a free gift of God's grace. Some delay because they do not want to repent of their sins just yet.

The word translated "found" in verse 16 implies a search before finding. The angel had not told the shepherds exactly where in Bethlehem that they would find the baby. Bethlehem at that time was not large, so it would not have taken the shepherds long to search the whole town. Their visit to Bethlehem confirmed that what the angel had told them was true. The Messiah indeed had come to redeem his people. They were not mistaken. It had not been a dream or a hallucination. They had seen it for themselves.

God does speak to all of us. He has given us his word, the Bible. In it we find the good news of salvation and God's guidance for our lives. How do we respond to it? Do we respond with scepticism and question whether God has really spoken to us? Do we hesitate or respond immediately? Do we act on what we have read and heard, or do we think that God must be speaking to someone else? God does offer his grace freely without cost, but he also requires us to respond to his offer. God does guide us through his Word and by his Holy Spirit, but he also requires us to respond to his guidance. Will you respond to him today?

The shepherds were not only the first witnesses of the gospel, they were also the first preachers of it. Verse 17 says, "When they had seen him, they spread the word concerning what had been told to them about this child." Having seen the baby themselves, they now had evidence enough that would satisfy others. Now the hush of wondering expectancy fell on all who heard what the shepherds said. Evidently, people listened to these shepherds even though they came from a despised class of society. Perhaps the people to whom they spoke were from the lower classes as well.

Even though God had broken into their lives and intervened in human history, the shepherds went back to work at their ordinary jobs. They returned to the fields. However, they returned as changed men. Verse 20 says, "The shepherds returned, glorifying and praising God for all the things they had heard and seen, which was just as they had been told."

They were full of praise to God for the news that they had heard and the sight that had confirmed it.

It is the duty of the redeemed to proclaim to others what they have seen and heard. The shepherds were not learned men. They were not eloquent speakers or persuasive salesman, but they could still tell others about what they had seen and heard. They could still give honour to God and celebrate his praises. There are few Billy Graham types in this world. Not everyone can be a powerful evangelist. However, most of the people who have come forward at Billy Graham crusades were brought there by someone else.

The gospel was meant for common, ordinary people like us. It was for simple folk that Jesus came to Earth to die. The shepherds were from a despised class of people, but the angel came to them with good news of great joy. They did not have a glamourous job, but they were faithful at it. They were alert and watchful when the good news came. When they heard the word, they responded immediately with enthusiasm and haste. They searched out the town of Bethlehem and saw the child that had been promised. Then they told others the good news and worshipped and praised God. We need more men and women like the shepherds. While they were common men, their attitudes were not so common.

Chapter 17

The Eyes of Faith
(Luke 2:21-35)

In this passage of scripture we see the inspired reaction of Simeon to Mary and Joseph bringing their son into the temple. We know nothing about Simeon apart from this story. His name was a common one, and attempts to identify him as a priest or an important person are without foundation. We seem to always think of him as an old man, but there is nothing in the account to suggest this except for his cheerful readiness to die.

Although Simeon was not apparently important or influential, he was special. Luke said that he was righteous. This means that he behaved well toward his fellow man. His actions were right. Obviously, he was not without sin. No one is. Devout is a translation of a Greek word that is used only by Luke in the New Testament. It means to hold well or carefully and, therefore, reverently and circumspectly. It signifies that Simeon was careful about his religious duties. Thus, Simeon was a man who was careful in the way that he lived in his life, and this showed both in his actions toward his fellow man and his observance of his religious duties. In this chapter it is clear that Simeon and Anna are representatives of real piety in a time of spiritual dearth and deadness.

Luke also said that the Holy Spirit was upon Simeon. This seems to mean that the Holy Spirit was on him continually. In the Old Testament, the Holy Spirit came on special people on special occasions for special reasons. The continuing presence of the Holy Spirit was rare. Simeon's endowment was special and we see here a foretaste of the continuing presence of the Holy Spirit in Christians. We also see another indication that Simeon was a deeply religious man who was close to God.

For me, the characteristic of Simeon that stands out the most was not the fact that he was righteous or devout. Although few people in his day were, he was not unique in that regard. The continuing presence of the Holy Spirit in his life made him stand out even amongst the devout. However, what made him stand out the most is his amazing faith.

Simeon's human eyes saw a tiny, seemingly ordinary human baby, being brought into the temple for a ritual that was supposed to be performed for every Jewish baby boy. However, his eyes of faith saw something entirely different.

Luke said that Simeon was waiting for the consolation of Israel. This is another way of saying that he was looking for the coming of the Messiah. The coming of the Messiah was expected to be preceded by a time of great suffering. The Messiah would then bring comfort to the nation of Israel. Thus, he would be the consolation of Israel. In days when the nation was oppressed, men of faith looked all the more intensely for the deliverer who would solve their problems. Israel, in Simeon's day, was oppressed. The Romans ruled over them.

There was no Jew who did not regard his nation as the chosen people. Scripture had plainly declared that to them. However, while they had enjoyed some time of relative prominence during the time of David and Solomon, throughout much of their history, the Jews had been threatened, oppressed, conquered and even exiled from their promised land. Thus, they looked forward to a new David who would restore them to a place of prominence. This was the Messianic hope.

While Simeon may or may not have had the same Messianic hope as many of his fellow Jews, he certainly had a strong messianic hope. When many of his contemporaries may have given up and thought of the Messiah as not coming at all, or as coming at some distant time in the future, Simeon knew that the Messiah was coming soon. In fact, the Holy Spirit had revealed to him that he would come during his lifetime. We are not told how the Holy Spirit spoke to him. It may have been a dream, a vision or some other kind of revelation. That does not matter.

What we are told is that, in fulfilment of that promise, Simeon was led by the Holy Spirit into the temple at the same time as Joseph and Mary came to officially present Jesus to God. Evidently Simeon was sensitive to the leading of the Spirit. We are also told that Simeon took the baby Jesus in his arms and praised God. He offered up a prayer of thanksgiving. A baby being officially presented to the Lord was not a rare event at that time. Today, many people who are not really devout will take their children to church to have them christened. It would not have been that much different in Simeon's day. Jesus was probably not even the only child in the temple that day. However, somehow Simeon recognized a baby boy as his long promised Messiah. We are told in Isaiah that there was nothing special about Jesus' appearance. The only way that Simeon could have known that Jesus was his Messiah was through the eyes of faith. Yet he clearly did recognize him as such.

Jesus did not look like a king. Indeed, his parents were poor, as their offering shows. He was not a person of influence, power or prestige. As a baby he certainly did not speak with authority as he did in his adult life. He performed no miracles. In short, Simeon's human eyes would not have seen anything special about Jesus, but his eyes of faith did. His human eyes saw a helpless baby boy. His eyes of faith saw a long promised Messiah.

It is interesting that there are two possible translations of verse 29. It could read, "Sovereign Lord, as you have promised, you now dismiss your servant in peace," or "... as you have promised, now dismiss... " As you can see, where you place the word, "now," does change the meaning somewhat. However, in either case, Simeon's "now" is significant. He is ready to die in peace *"now"* that he has seen God's salvation. Actually, Simeon did not literally see God's salvation. What he saw was the baby through whom God, in time, would bring salvation. He saw through the eyes of faith the future salvation of his people.

The language that Simeon used is that of a freed slave. He actually called himself God's slave. The word that is rendered servant is "doulous," which literally means slave. Simeon may have been thinking of his death as his release from a long task. Many people at the end of life have thought that way, which has prompted some to think of Simeon as an old man, which may or may not have been the case.

Seeing the Messiah as the consolation of Israel and the Saviour of his people was a popular concept in Simeon's day. However, many of them had a different view of salvation than we do. Some would have thought of salvation as deliverance from oppression. They would remember Moses, the ten plagues and the crossing of the Red Sea. They would contemplate how God saved them from slavery. Others would be thinking of a great king like David who would lead them in victory over the armies of Rome. Either way, it was physical and not spiritual salvation that would be on their minds. They would be like people today who preach a social gospel or some form of liberation theology. We must not be too hasty to condemn them for that kind of thinking. There are many prophecies in the Old Testament that can easily be interpreted that way.

Our hindsight enables us to see God's salvation of his people in a different light. We know that Jesus came to suffer and die for our sins. We know that, on Calvary, he paid the price of our justification. We know that he redeemed us from slavery to sin and death and set us free from Satan.

Whether you view the Messiah as a miracle worker like Moses, or a conquering king like David, or a vicarious Saviour like Jesus actually came to be, it is hard to see a baby fulfilling that role. Babies do not perform miracles as Moses and Jesus did. Babies do not reign on thrones as David, or in the hearts of people as Jesus did. Babies do not offer themselves up as sacrificial lambs as Jesus did. When Simeon saw Jesus as the Saviour of his people, he saw him that way through the eyes of faith. Whether or not Simeon fully understood how Jesus was going to save his people does not matter. What matters is that Simeon saw the future through the eyes of faith and in that future he saw the salvation of his people.

It is interesting that Simeon did not restrict the salvation that Jesus would bring to Israel. He said God prepared his salvation "in the sight of all people". This is clear enough, but Simeon went on to say, "a light for revelation to the Gentiles and glory for your people Israel." Simeon definitely thought of God's salvation as coming not to one nation alone, but to all people everywhere.

Because the Jews considered themselves to be the people of God, some thought that they were bound to be masters of the world and lords of the nations. Since this was not in harmony with their actual status as an oppressed people, they looked forward to a time of radical change. Some thought that a great celestial champion would descend to Earth to lead them in victory. Others thought that a great king would arise out of David's line and bring back the days of glory. Still others believed that God himself would break into history in some supernatural way to put the people of Israel into their proper place.

In contrast to all those ideas of conquest and victory, there were a few people who were known as *the Quiet in the Land*. They had no dreams of violence and power. They had no thoughts of victorious armies. Instead, they spent their days in constant prayer and quiet watching for God to come. They lived their lives waiting quietly and patiently upon God. Simeon was like that in prayer, in worship, and in humble and faithful expectation. He was waiting for the day when God would come and comfort his people.

Simeon was not a zealot who wanted to crush the Romans. He was not a nationalist who wanted Israel to rule the nations. He did not see the Messiah as coming to restore the kingdom to Israel, as even the disciples of Jesus saw him. Instead he saw the Messiah as "a light for revelation to the Gentiles." The worldwide mission of the Messiah comes out clearly in the early chapters of Luke.

Simeon, through the eyes of faith, saw the baby Jesus as the light of the world. John, writing in retrospect, saw Jesus the same way. He said in John 1:9, "The true light that gives light to every man was coming into the world." Jesus clearly saw himself as the light of the world. He came to shed light on our hearts and reveal our innermost thoughts and feelings. Simeon, through the eyes of faith, somehow knew that. He said that through Jesus "the thoughts of many hearts will be revealed."

When Simeon, with the eyes of faith, praised God for what Jesus was going to do, Joseph and Mary marvelled. Every parent is astonished and pleased when others see wonderful things in their children. Even though the shepherds had come to pay homage to the baby Jesus, they still had not said the things about him that Simeon had prophesied. Mary and Joseph must also have wondered how Simeon could have known all that he did. There is no record that he was visited by an angel choir or anything like that.

However, when Simeon had blessed the couple he had other things to say about Jesus. We now find that the whole story is not sweetness and light. Salvation will be purchased for the people of God. That is true. However, that purchase price will be costly indeed and Simeon sombrely related this to the mother of Jesus. Light not only reveals the beautiful things of the world, it reveals the ugly things as well. Simeon predicted that Jesus would be a stumbling block to many people. Some people love darkness rather than light.

Jesus is the magnet of the ages. He draws some and repels others. He drew and still draws much opposition. Toward Jesus there can be no neutrality. We can either surrender to him or be at war with him. Unfortunately, pride often prevents us from the surrender that leads to victory. When people saw Jesus suffer, their reaction showed on which side they stood. They either rejoiced in their apparent victory or mourned at their apparent defeat. Naturally, Jesus' suffering did not leave his mother untouched. Simeon knew this in advance and warned her that a sword would pierce her soul. She was at the cross to watch her son die as a criminal. Such a sight would have devastated any mother.

Simeon predicted that Jesus would cause many to rise and many to fall. He knew that the light that Jesus brought to the world would shed light on things that some would rather have left in darkness. The ministry of Jesus forced people to make a choice. Some chose the way of repentance and faith. Others chose the path of pride and disbelief. People still make these choices today.

While many saw the Messiah as a conquering hero, Simeon, through the eyes of faith, saw Jesus as the suffering servant of God. He saw that our salvation would be costly and Jesus' ministry would be a stumbling block to many. How much Mary understood of what Simeon said to her, we do not know. His words must have seemed out of place in the midst of the glorious things that had been spoken about her son. However, we now know that they were fulfilled.

Simeon's human eyes may have been old and feeble. That is quite possible, although not certain. However, it is certain that his eyes of faith were in great shape. Through the eyes of faith he saw a tiny baby's future. He saw Jesus as his Messiah. He saw Jesus as the saviour of his people. He saw Jesus as the light of the world. He saw Jesus as the suffering servant of God. How do you see Jesus? In what shape are your eyes of faith? Just as it was in Jesus' day, you cannot be neutral. Jesus will reveal your inner thoughts and motives. How will you respond to that light? Are your eyes of faith old and feeble or sharp and clear?

Chapter 18
An Old Woman and A Young Baby
(Luke 2:36-40)

For the last several chapters we have been looking at people who encountered the baby Jesus. We started looking at Elizabeth who met Jesus while he was still in Mary's womb. Elizabeth was upright, humble, especially blessed by God. Then we thought about Joseph, the man who God had ordained to be Jesus' earthly father. Joseph was kind as well as being a man of faith and a man of action. Then we dealt with the shepherds who came to see Jesus while he was still in the manger. They were faithful, responsive and worshipful. We examined Simeon as a man who, through the eyes of faith, saw the baby Jesus as his Messiah, the Saviour of his people and the light of the world. In this chapter, let us look at Anna who also encountered Jesus as a tiny baby.

Luke records that Anna's encounter with Jesus immediately followed Simeon's. To Simeon's prophecy he adds the thanksgiving of another representative of organized religion. Anna was a prophetess. Elizabeth was the wife of a priest. Anna, like Simeon, was one of the Quiet in the Land. While many religious people failed to accept Jesus, this early recognition came from those who were actually faithful in following the requirements of their religion.

Nothing more is known about Anna than what we read here. However, even in these few verses, Luke has drawn a complete character sketch. We know little about her, but we know enough.

The first thing that Luke tells us about Anna is that she was a prophetess. There had been no known prophet in Israel for hundreds of years, so it is noteworthy that God raised up this prophetess. Also, according to the Talmud, the Jews counted seven prophetesses, so this was no ordinary distinction. This, of course, means that she was especially called and gifted by God.

We also learn that Anna was the daughter of Phanuel, of whom we know nothing, and that she was from the tribe of Asher. Asher was one of the so called lost ten tribes. Evidently some members of it survived and kept their genealogies.

Anna was very old. It is not clear whether she was in fact 84 years old or whether she had been a widow for that length of time. If the latter was the case, then she would have been very old. Monefiore made it 106 years. She would have likely been 15 when she was married, married for 7 years, and widowed for 84. However, even if she was only 84, that would make her a very old woman at that time.

Anna was a widow and had been so for some time. She was also too old to get married. She had known sorrow and had not grown bitter. Sorrow can do one of two things for us. It can make us hard, bitter, resentful and rebellious against God or it can make us kinder, softer and more sympathetic. It can despoil us of our faith or it can root our faith even deeper. It all depends upon our view of God. If we view God as a cruel tyrant, then we will turn away from him when sorrow hits us. If we view God as a loving Father, then we will turn to him for comfort and strength when sorrow hits us.

Luke says that Anna never left the temple. This could either mean that she had quarters within the temple precincts or that she was constantly at worship there. The latter is more likely. It seems that she was always there. The Holy Spirit kept her in the temple just as he led Simeon to the temple. We have here a picture of faithfulness. Anna never missed a temple service. Not many of us could say that. We are very good at finding excuses for skipping services.

Anna not only regularly attended the public worship services; she was also engaged in private worship. Fasting and praying, practices which could be performed by individuals quite apart from corporate worship, point to a disciplined life. Anna was a faithful servant of God. She served him night and day, day after day, for many years.

Not all of us are called to God's special service. Few of us will be a prophet or a prophetess. However, all of us can be faithful. We can faithfully serve God at what he has called us to do. This is fundamentally important. If we read the Bible, we can easily see that God places a high priority on faithfulness. Will God say of you, "Well done, good and faithful servant."?

Luke said that Anna spent her time in God's house with God's people. We rob ourselves of a priceless treasure when we neglect to be one with God's worshipping people. Anna was worshipful. She worshipped God corporately and privately. Public worship is great, but private worship is also great. Someone once said, "They pray best together who first pray alone."

Anna came at the critical moment and thanked God, presumably for sending the Messiah. The word that is translated as coming up is often used for suddenly bursting in. However, here it probably means coming up and standing by and so hearing Simeon's wonderful words so that her words form a kind of footnote to his. Anna was deeply moved hearing that the Messiah had finally come to redeem his people and she kept repeating his thanksgiving. Luke, however, gives no indication of the content of her thanksgiving, nor of the further comments of Anna.

We are also not told whether Anna recognized for herself that the baby Jesus was the long promised Messiah or if she simply responded to what Simeon had said. In either case it involves a step of faith and responding to the prompting of the Holy Spirit. It was obviously no coincidence that Anna came into that part of the temple at that particular moment.

Anna was worshipful. She spent much time in the temple worshipping God both publicly and privately. Because she was continually in the house of God she received a unique blessing. She was able to see the Messiah. If we spend much time worshipping God, then we too will receive a blessing. Like Anna, this blessing will probably come suddenly and unexpectedly.

Anna could not keep this blessing to herself. She simply had to tell others. Luke said she "spoke about the child to all who were looking forward to the redemption of Israel" (verse 38). The redemption of Israel is another way of referring to the deliverance to be effected by the Messiah. Evidently there was a group of people at that time who were waiting expectantly for the coming of the Messiah. These like minded people were either gathered around Anna and Simeon or were people that Anna met from time to time in the temple. There was a nucleus of Old Testament saints who were prepared for the coming of the Messiah when he at last appeared in Jerusalem. When Jesus reached maturity and began his ministry, these people had probably all passed away, but they had their hour of hope and joy. There were many who were not so prepared. When Herod asked the scholars about the birthplace of the Messiah, it appears that not one of them went to Bethlehem to check out whether it had indeed happened. When Jesus later performed miracles in their midst, they said that he must be from Satan.

Anna was old and still had hope. Age can take away the bloom and strength of our bodies, but it can do worse – the years can take away the life of our hearts until the hopes that we cherished die and we become dully content and grimly resigned to things as they are. Again this all depends on how we think of God. If we think of him as distant and detached, then we may despair. However, if we think of him as intimately connected with life and deeply concerned about his children, then we may be sure that the best is yet to be and the years will never kill our hope. The years had left Anna without bitterness and with an unshakable hope because she kept her contact with him who is the source of strength and in whose strength our weakness is made perfect.

Chapter 19
God In Her Womb
(Luke 1:39-56)

The story of Jesus' birth is a simple one. We are given very few details as to what actually happened. This is to prevent the human interest aspects from overshadowing the central truth which was, of course, that God became a human being to live for a while among us. Think of how the media dwells on the intimate details of the lives of celebrities.

Mary was betrothed to a humble workman, Joseph, whom we have already studied. Both Joseph and Mary were of the royal line of David, but both were poor. There is nothing attractive about the birth of Jesus. As Isaiah 53 says, there was nothing about him that would ordinarily draw people toward him.

In this passage of scripture, we read that Mary left her home in Nazareth soon after she received the news from the angel Gabriel that she was going to have a son and that her relative, Elizabeth, was already pregnant. When Elizabeth greeted her, it was no ordinary welcome that she received. Elizabeth's salutation was that of a mother to a mother, the mother of the preparer to the mother of the one for whom he would prepare the way. As you might remember, Elizabeth burst into song when her baby leaped in the womb. Mary responded by bursting into song as well. However, while Elizabeth's words were excited and tumultuous, Mary's were calm and measured. It would seem that, along the journey to Elizabeth's house, Mary spent some time contemplating the news that she had received from Gabriel and its implications.

The song of Mary is called the Magnificat from its opening words in the Latin translation. It is an exclamation of praise in Old Testament language. There are quite a number of resemblances to Hannah's song in 1 Samuel 2:1-10. It is possible that Mary was meditating on that passage during her journey. However, there is a difference in tone. Hannah's song was a shout of triumph over her enemies. Mary's song was a humble contemplation of the mercies of God.

There are social revolutionary statements in Mary's song. God casts down the mighty and exalts the humble. There are economic revolutionary statements in it. God fills the hungry and sends the rich away empty.

We do not know how much Mary understood about who the baby in her womb was. Did she really know that the One who created the universe was growing inside her? However, we do know this incredible truth. Mary's song tells much about what God is like. She praises him for who he is and what he does.

Mary began by praising God. There is synonymous parallelism here and we should not try to distinguish between soul and spirit or between praising and rejoicing. By referring to God as her Saviour, she recognized her need. She was a sinner in need of salvation like everyone else. She knew that she was a poor, ordinary young woman who had been uniquely blessed by God and so she referred both to her humble state and to the fact that future generations would acknowledge God's blessing upon her. Literally, the passage says that God has looked upon the low or humble condition of his servant. Notwithstanding her humble rank and her poverty, God showed Mary favour. Remember that her response to Gabriel's announcement was, "I am the Lord's servant." (Luke 1:38). She saw herself as insignificant, but that did not matter, for the Mighty One was at work.

God is not a respecter of persons. He is not influenced to confer favours by wealth or office. He seeks out the humble and contrite and imparts rich blessings to those who feel that they need them and will bless him for them. Jesus made this clear in the Sermon on the Mount when he said, "Blessed are the poor in spirit... " (Matthew 5:3) and "Blessed are those who hunger and thirst after righteousness" (Matthew 5:6).

From thankfulness for what God has done for her, Mary turned to contemplation of God himself. She dwelt on three things: his power, his holiness and his mercy. Mercy refers to favour shown to the miserable and guilty. It continues and abounds. Mary may be looking back to specific occasions in the past when God had done the things that she enumerates. She did speak in the past tense. However, it is more likely that she was looking forward in a spirit of prophecy. Old Testament prophets often used the past tense when foretelling what God would do in the future. The idea was that what God had prophesied through his prophet was so certain of its fulfilment that it could be spoken of as having already taken place. Of course, since God is the same yesterday, today and forever, the mercy that he has shown in the past, he will show in the future.

God blesses the humble. He bestows his goodness to the poor in spirit. He forgives the repentant and contrite of their sins. He shows his favour to those who know that they need it. He heaps his rewards on those who hunger and thirst after righteousness. Unfortunately, very few people are genuinely humble like Mary. Most of us think that we deserve the good things that happen to us. We may even think that we deserve more.

The first section of Mary's song tells of a complete reversal of human values. It is not the proud or the mighty or the rich who are blessed by God. Indeed, through his Messiah, God is about to overthrow all of these. True Christianity puts an end to the world's labels and prestige. God scatters those who are proud in their innermost thoughts. Notice the consistent biblical emphasis, particularly in the New Testament, on attitudes and thoughts instead of actions. Most of us think of pride as bragging to others about our accomplishments. However, we all know that pride begins in the mind. True Christianity is the death of pride. We may be proud of how much better we think we are than those around us, but if we compare ourselves to Jesus Christ, then we cannot help but be humbled.

Mary sang about God bringing down rulers from their thrones. She was obviously speaking about people who were actually ruling, and not just powerful people. Throughout history, God has brought down many powerful empires and kings. In our study of Daniel, we were reminded of that.

There is also a revolutionary note about filling the hungry and sending the rich away empty. In the ancient world, it was accepted that the rich would be well cared for and poor people must expect to go hungry. People viewed wealth as an obvious sign of God's favour and poverty and disease as an obvious sign of God's displeasure. That is why the disciples asked Jesus who sinned when they encountered a man born blind. That is also why Job's friends accused Job of great sin. However, Mary sang of a God who is not bound by what we think or see. He sees inside the hearts of men and women. He turns human attitudes and the orders of society upside down.

God often does things exactly the opposite of what we would expect. God scatters the proud and blesses the humble. He brings down the powerful and mighty and exalts the lowly. He fills the hungry with good things and sends the rich away empty.

After singing of God turning man's values upside down, Mary now sang of his help for his people. This reminds us of God's mercy towards Abraham and Israel. Mary said that God's revolutionary action fulfilled through the coming of the Messiah is not so much a completely new thing as a continuation of his mercy to Abraham. It is also in accordance with his promises to the patriarchs.

We know that many prophecies were fulfilled with the birth of Jesus Christ. His virgin birth and his birthplace are two of the more obvious ones. We also know that many more were fulfilled with his crucifixion and resurrection. Mary's song reminds us that God is faithful. He will keep his promises. Some of them might take hundreds of years to fulfill, but that is but an instant in eternity. Just as God is not bound by human values, he is also not bound by human time lines.

However, while we are assured that God will keep his promises, we must also be aware that he will keep them in his own way and in his own time. Remember that the biblical scholars of Jesus' day knew the Messianic promises very well, but they still did not recognize their Messiah when he walked among them. Because he did not fulfill the promises in the way that they expected them to be fulfilled, they attributed his miracles to Satan and they crucified him as a blasphemer. Let us not make the same mistake. Many people throughout history have predicted when and how Jesus would return, and they have all been mistaken. Some of them have brought considerable hardship to their followers.

Chapter 20
Blinded, So That He Could See
(Acts 9:1-19)

Some of the encounters that we studied would be classified as theophanies, appearances of God. Many people believe that the theophanies that are recorded in the Old Testament are records of pre-incarnate appearances of Jesus Christ. Thus, they would be encounters with God, the Son, rather than God, the Father. This could be true, but we have no way of knowing and it does not really matter.

In any case, in this chapter we are looking at a post-incarnate manifestation of Christ. He revealed himself in some way to Saul on the road to Damascus. This encounter with Jesus dramatically changed him. In fact, it has been called the most famous conversion story in history. This Saul who met Jesus Christ on the road to Damascus was probably the most zealous persecutor of Christians in his day. He later became the apostle Paul and it is this event that was the most significant step on that journey from persecutor to apostle. Paul made many references to this conversion experience. He mentioned it in 1 Corinthians 15:8f; Galatians 1:12-17; Philippians 3:4-7 and 1 Timothy 1:12-16. These passages describe the way in which Paul had been a persecutor of the church, but had a vision of Jesus. As a result of this vision, he was called to be an apostle and summoned to preach to Gentiles.

This account in Acts is Luke's record of what happened that day. He probably got the story from Paul since he was a frequent companion of Paul's in his latter journeys. We know that Luke was a careful historian. Luke also recorded Paul relating the story twice. He evidently attached great importance to the story of Saul's conversion as the turning point not simply in the career of a man, Paul, but also as a pivotal event in the history of Christianity.

We would view it as a very significant event as well. It is also a very interesting story. When someone undergoes such a radical transformation, it is worth studying what happened to him. We do like to listen to stories of people who were saved from a life of sin and degradation. Saul was not a notorious sinner, but his conversion was far more dramatic than most stories that we will ever hear. When we study the story of Saul's conversion, we must not make the mistake of thinking that it was normal. Luke recorded many conversions in Acts, and none of them were like Saul's. His was the exception to the rule. Let us look at the story. Let us study Saul's transformation.

The first time we meet Saul who later became known as Paul, he is present at the stoning of Stephen, the first Christian martyr. Acts 7:58 says, "Meanwhile, the witnesses laid their clothes at the feet of a young man named Saul." This may sound like Saul was a mere observer, which was definitely not the case. Acts 8:1 says that Saul gave approval to the stoning of Stephen. Verse three says that he began to destroy the church. He went from house to house, dragging off men and women and putting them in prison. This persecution that Saul led prompted many Christians to flee Jerusalem. These scattered Christians preached the gospel wherever they went. Thus, Saul was used by God to spread the gospel even when he was still in opposition to it. This is another example of the sovereignty of God. He uses people in ways that they are not even aware of.

Saul was not content to just persecute Christians in Jerusalem. The implication is that he was not satisfied with the results of his campaign in Jerusalem and he was anxious to do more. He knew that many had fled the city and he did not want them to escape his clutches. He went to the high priest and asked for letters to the synagogues in Damascus. He probably had heard that many Christians had fled there. Saul was determined to pursue them there and bring them back to Jerusalem as prisoners. Damascus would have been a likely place for the early Christians to run to. It was one of the oldest cities in the world. It was an important town with a large and influential Jewish population. Since most of the early Christians were Jewish, it would have been an attractive place for them. Note that there was more than one Jewish synagogue in Damascus. This was one indication of the size of the city and the size of the Jewish population there. Whether or not Saul had the authority to execute Christians is questionable. It would seem that only the Romans had that power. However, they had granted some powers to the Jewish religious authorities and it may be that Saul was only asking for permission to arrest Christians. That he wanted them put to death is clear from his actions towards Stephen and Acts 9:1, as well as other references in Acts. If Saul overstepped his authority by authorizing the stoning of Stephen and seeking the death of other Christians, we should not be surprised. Many people in the past have taken advantage of their position and overstepped their authority and many people still do this today.

The description of Christians as followers of the Way is peculiar to Acts. It could be Luke's way of referring to Christianity as the way of truth. It could be a reference to Jesus calling himself the Way. We must remember that at that time, Christianity was considered to be an offshoot or sect of Judaism. Some Samaritans had come to believe through the ministry of Philip, but Samaritans were still half Jewish. Cornelius' conversion came later. Thus, Luke may be saying that the early Christians were Jews who served God in a different way than other Jews. This was what upset Saul. We do not know what contact, if any, that Saul would have had with Jesus while he was still alive, but we do know that he would have considered him to be a blasphemer and a false Messiah. He certainly considered his followers to be heretics. Saul was a Pharisee. This was the most legalistic group of Jews in that day. He was a meticulous follower of the law as he understood it. The law clearly declared the blasphemers should be stoned. That is why Saul was instrumental in having Stephen stoned and that is why he wanted to go to Damascus to arrest Christians. He thought that he was following the law of God.

Damascus was about 140 miles (about 220 kilometres) from Jerusalem. To us that does not sound like a large distance at all. However, we travel by car and by plane. Most of the travel in that day was by foot. It would have taken Saul about one week to reach Damascus. This is a further indication of Saul's resoluteness. He was willing to go to great lengths to arrest Christians. He was certain that many of them had escaped there and he was hot on their trail.

Saul was zealous. Of that there can be no doubt. He went to great lengths to follow what he thought was the will of God. That he was horribly wrong, we all know from hindsight. However, we must not think that we are not in danger of making the same mistake. Many people throughout history have done strange things in the name of God. The Spanish Inquisition comes to mind. Apartheid in South Africa and segregation in the southern United States are other notable examples of people committing atrocities in the name of Christ. What about the Crusades? We must never think that we are immune to the type of distorted thinking that believes that hatred and violence can be compatible with true belief in Jesus Christ. We must examine our own hearts to check for the seeds of bitterness and hatred toward others. We must check for that vindictive spirit that can destroy us.

As he neared Damascus, at about noon, without any previous warning, Saul found himself surrounded by an intensely bright light and heard a voice speaking to him. This bright light must be understood as an expression of divine glory. Since we know that no man can see God, it is understandable that the effect of the light was to cause blindness. The voice is also a common characteristic of divine revelation. We see this in

Exodus 3:1-6 and Isaiah 6:8. Here, however, it is not the voice of God, the Father, but of Jesus. Saul can be said to have had an encounter with the risen Jesus Christ, in which he heard his voice.

However, while we know the identity of the one who was speaking to Saul, apparently he did not. "Lord," is the normal reverential address that one might be expected to use in addressing a heavenly figure. Saul knew that he was experiencing some kind of divine revelation, but he might have thought that he was addressing an angel or some other heavenly being. It is significant that Saul had to ask the identity of the speaker.

This was not an ordinary appearance of the risen Jesus Christ like the ones that he made to his disciples between his resurrection and his ascension. When Paul listed the appearances of Jesus in 1 Corinthians 15 he said, "and last of all he appeared to me also, as one abnormally born." (verse 8). It seems that Jesus did not take on bodily form on this occasion. He simply manifested himself as a bright light and a voice.

Evidently, revelation was given to Saul alone. His companions heard a voice, but saw no one. We also know from Acts 22 that they could not make out what the voice was saying. Jesus was not speaking to them, but to Saul alone. Nevertheless, they were witnesses that something decidedly unusual had happened to Saul. Saul's instinctive reaction when confronted by such a brilliant light was to close his eyes. When he opened them he discovered that he was blind. He had to be led into the city of Damascus. His blindness was proof that something dramatic had happened to him. He had not experienced some kind of hallucination, but had had an encounter with the risen Christ. There were even witnesses to his experience.

It is interesting that Jesus simply identified himself and told Saul to go into the city to await further instructions. At that time he did not tell Saul what he had in mind for him. We know from history what it was. Saul became the great apostle Paul. Paul took the gospel of Christ to many places where people had not heard of him.

The statement, "I am Jesus, whom you are persecuting" (Acts 9:5) is significant. By persecuting Christians, Saul was persecuting Jesus Christ. Anything done to a follower of Jesus is, in effect, done to Jesus himself. We also see that from Matthew 25:40 where Jesus said, "I tell you the truth, whatever you did for one of the least of these brothers of mine, you did for me." Saul's misguided zeal for God had turned into an attack on God, who had raised Jesus from the dead.

We are not told that Saul prayed "the sinner's prayer". As I mentioned previously, this was an unusual conversion experience, perhaps even a unique one. The surrender to the will of Christ was the conversion of Saul. There is no formula for becoming a Christian. Every encounter with God is different. Some people have a dramatic conversion experience.

Some do not. Some are saved from a wicked and wayward life. Some grow up in a Christian home and decide very early in life to follow Jesus. God is quite capable of dealing with different people in different ways.

Saul met Jesus on the road to Damascus and that encounter changed his life forever. Have you met him? Your encounter with him would be different than Saul's, but if you meet Jesus, then your life will be changed as well. You cannot meet him and remain the same. He has a powerful effect upon people. They either turn to him or turn away from him.

It is obvious that the experience on the road had a dramatic effect on Saul. His blindness is one evidence of that. Luke also recorded that Saul did not eat or drink anything for three days. He was likely overcome by shock and remorse. His penitence showed that he realised the enormity of his actions in persecuting Christians. He experienced real guilt and anguish. These three days must have been a time of terrible stress and strain. However, relief was sent to him. God prepared someone to meet his need of forgiveness. A disciple was prepared to go and meet him and convey to him both healing for his blindness and baptism as a Christian. This arrangement was confirmed by a double vision. Divine instructions were clearly given to show the divine choice of Saul as God's instrument.

An otherwise unknown disciple by the name of Ananias was in Damascus. Beyond doubt, Ananias stands out as one of the forgotten heroes of the church. Ananias received a vision from God and was told to go to Saul. The message must have sounded mad to Ananias. The name of Saul was not unknown to him and his reaction was understandable and his remarks entirely natural. He had heard many reports about him and he knew why Saul had journeyed to Damascus. His comments showed the incredible nature of Saul's conversion. Ananias, in his ignorance, saw only a man with an evil reputation. Jesus saw in Saul a man transformed by grace.

Ananias was obedient to his vision. He might well have approached Saul with suspicion. He might well have begun with recriminations. Many of us would have. However, instead he began with the words, "Brother Saul." All suspicion had vanished and Ananias took Saul to heart as a brother in Christ. What a welcome was there! What a gracious word, "Brother." This is one of the sublimest examples of Christian love. Ananias was able to forgive the very man that had come to arrest him and his fellow disciples.

Ananias laid hands on Saul. This is understood as a symbolic act of healing and Saul's sight was immediately restored. Then it appears that Ananias, and not an apostle, baptized Saul. This together with Ananias' greeting showed Saul's full initiation into the Christian church. There is no long period of testing for this former enemy. Saul's repentance had been proven genuine. He had met Christ and had come to faith in him. No further delay was necessary.

It is very important that Ananias came to meet Saul after his conversion. Unfortunately, that does not always happen today. We would never abandon a baby shortly after birth. That is considered the height of cruelty. However, we do not show the same hesitancy in abandoning babes in Christ. New Christians need to be welcomed into the fold. They need to be nurtured and instructed. They may not always turn out to be apostle Pauls, but who knows?

The apostle Paul's conversion to Christianity was sudden and dramatic. He was zealous for God and tried to serve God by persecuting Christians. He was ignorant and misguided. Unfortunately, the world is full of people like that. Many try to serve God out of ignorance. Even some who call themselves Christians think that they are serving God even when they are in error. Saul met Christ. He was blinded by him so that he might see the truth. Sometimes that is what it takes. God will go to great lengths to get his message across. Saul did sincerely repent and his life was turned around. Fortunately, he was helped along the path by Ananias. He was welcomed into the family of God as a brother in Christ. What a wonderful story! Most of us will never be anything like the apostle Paul. However, we can be like the disciple, Ananias. We can welcome and encourage new Christians. This wonderful story can be repeated if we are willing to be used by God.

Chapter 21
Do Not Be Afraid!
(Revelation 1: 9-20)

The last recorded appearance of Jesus Christ occurs in the book of Revelation. This is a difficult book to understand because it is full of symbolism and we cannot always be certain of the meaning of the symbols. Revelation belongs to a class of literature known as apocalyptic. In fact, the name "Revelation" is translated from the Greek word "apocalupsis" which means "to uncover, to unveil". Thus, the book of Revelation is meant to uncover something that is hidden. It is the supernatural revelation of divine truth.

A great deal of apocalyptic literature has been written. Ezekiel, Zechariah and Daniel are examples of Old Testament apocalyptic literature. Also, there was a great deal of Jewish apocalyptic literature written after the Old Testament was completed. Notable examples are the books of Enoch and the Assumption of Moses. Jesus also spoke in apocalyptic terms on occasions (Matthew 24, 25). However, Revelation is the only apocalyptic book in the New Testament.

The reason for the apocalyptic style of writing is usually severe persecution. The people of God are oppressed and feel defeated. Their future, from a human point of view, looks hopeless. The writer encourages them by saying that God is in control and their enemies will be defeated. However, he writes in code. He uses symbols so only those who know the code will understand. This would effectively hide his message from those who would persecute God's people.

Revelation was addressed to the seven churches of the Roman province of Asia, an area that is now known as Turkey. The usual form of introduction used in the ancient world in writing letters was used. Though some have taken these seven churches as representing seven successive periods of church history, there is no hint of such an interpretation in the book itself. The seven churches addressed were all literal churches in existence at that time. Unfortunately, now the area is Islamic with precious little Christian presence. John wrote to these churches to assure them of their final salvation at the end of the age.

The book of Revelation portrays the unseen world that lies behind what is going on in the visible world. It pictures a church that is far from infallible, plagued with heresies and sometimes blighted with apostasy, but still in the omnipotent hand of the eternal Lord of the universe.

This book deals with the second coming of Christ. This is an event which will make manifest the sovereignty of God that is not clearly seen today. The return of the Lord is spoken of as a public, visible event: "every eye will see him" (1:7). Through John, God communicated to the persecuted Christians that the One that they called Lord would eventually be revealed as Lord.

The events of the book of Revelation took place on the isle of Patmos. This is a barren, rocky island about ten miles (sixteen kilometres) long and five miles (eight kilometres) wide. It is an obscure island of little significance, yet on this island some key events took place.

John referred to himself as a brother and companion in suffering. He addressed his readers as one who shared with them the tribulation and the kingdom. These two themes – the tribulation of God's people and the coming of the kingdom – run throughout the book of Revelation.

John was banished to the remote island of Patmos by the Romans because of his Christian witness. He was an exile, "because of the word of God and the testimony of Jesus." John was charged with sedition because he preached the gospel. At that time, emperor worship was enforced upon the subjects of the Roman Empire. They had to confess Caesar as Lord and worship him as a god. This was something that no Christian could do. To a Christian there is only one Lord and only one God. Thus, for John to preach the gospel of Christ was to preach disloyalty to the Roman government, and that was inexcusable. Therefore, John was banished as a political prisoner.

The situation looked hopeless for John. By then he was an old man. All of the other apostles had probably been killed for their testimony and now he was suffering for his. The situation did not look much better for his readers. The Christian church was very small and the Roman Empire was very large and powerful. How could this small remnant withstand an attack from such a powerful enemy?

Today, we Christians in North America do not usually suffer as much persecution for our faith as John and his readers did. However, the situation that we enjoy here and now is an exception to the general rule of history. True followers of Christ, those who boldly proclaim his name and preach his gospel usually suffer for their testimony. Jesus promised his followers persecution in John 16:33. Paul said in 2 Timothy 3:12, "In fact, everyone who wants to live a godly life in Christ Jesus will be persecuted." He also said in Acts 14:22, "We must go through many hardships to enter the kingdom of God." Tribulation and the kingdom go together. You cannot enter the kingdom unless you are willing to suffer tribulation.

Many people today preach an easy gospel. They promise a life of blessing to all who claim the name of Christ. They say health and wealth are the birthrights of the children of God. But, is this true? Jesus did not promise an easy life, but rather a hard one. He said in Matthew 10:38, 39: "And anyone who does not take his cross and follow me is not worthy of me. Whoever finds his life will lose it, and whoever loses his life for my sake will find it." If we would be true followers of Christ, then we must be willing to die for him. Christ did not promise that our problems would go away when we accepted him as Savior and Lord, but that they would increase.

If we are truly committed to Christ, then we are engaged in a battle against Satan and the forces of darkness. Satan is a formidable foe and he does not give up easily. However, we are promised the resources of God to help us win the victory over hardship and persecution. The path for Jesus was not easy. It led to a cross. It will not be easy for us to follow him, but we can triumph just as he triumphed.

There, on that lonely island, John saw a vision and heard a voice. It was the voice of Christ. He reassured John that he is the Alpha and Omega, the first and the last. Alpha is the first letter of the Greek alphabet and Omega is the last. Jesus told John that he is the beginning and the end, the Lord of all that happens in human history. He is in control.

John described his vision of Christ for us. He is "like a Son of man". This is a reference to Daniel 7:13. It was Jesus' favourite title for himself and shows his real humanity. The long garment suggests a personage of distinction – either a priest or a king. Jesus is, of course, both. The white hair suggests both age and holiness as well as wisdom. From Daniel 7:9 we can see that it also shows the deity of Christ. The flaming eyes tell us that Christ sees and knows all. The feet like brass and the voice are references to Daniel 10:6. The feet show the strength and speed of Christ and the voice shows that Christ's word goes out everywhere. The sword of his mouth is the sword of the Spirit which is the word of God. Ephesians 6:17 and Hebrews 4:12 talk of the power of the word of God. Just as God spoke and the world was created, so Christ speaks and it is done. His face shining as the sun is a picture of his exalted glory. It should remind us of the Transfiguration.

This vision took John's eyes off his desperate condition and turned them on his exalted Savior. As the song goes: "Turn your eyes upon Jesus, Look full in his wonderful face and the things of earth will go strangely dim in the light of his glory and grace." This is a lesson that we need to learn and remember. Whenever we focus on ourselves, we may become depressed and defeated. However, when we focus on Christ, we will be victorious.

John's immediate reaction when confronted with the risen Lord was to fall prostrate to the ground as though he were dead. This is a common reaction to the manifestation of divine glory. We can see the same reaction in Isaiah 6:5; Ezekiel 1:28 and Daniel 8:17. None but the pure in heart can see God and live. John's reaction of fear was quite normal.

John's fears were calmed. He was told to stop being afraid. He had nothing to fear because Jesus was in control. Jesus conquered death and is alive for evermore. The keys are symbols of authority. Not only did Jesus conquer death, but he has control over death. He has the power to raise us from the dead to live with him forever and ever. Christ's victory over death meant a great deal to the early Christian. The resurrection was the main focus of early Christian preaching. Unfortunately, the Christian church has drifted away from this emphasis.

We must note that John stayed on the isle of Patmos. His banishment did not end with his vision of Christ. His suffering continued. The only thing that changed was that his focus was shifted away from his suffering to his Lord. This alone calmed his fears. He was told that, despite the bleak outlook, God was in control. This is the main message of the book of Revelation. "Do not be afraid." Things may look bad, but this is because we do not see what is going on behind the scenes. We do not see the working of God.

We are not promised an easy way but rather a rough road, a life of trouble. We will suffer for our faith if we are bold in the proclamation of the gospel. But Jesus is with us in our suffering to give us victory over our suffering. We have nothing to fear because we are in his control. The kingdom awaits us if we are willing to suffer tribulation. Paul says in Romans 8:17, 18: "Now if we are children, then we are heirs – heirs of God and coheirs with Christ, if indeed we share in his sufferings in order that we may also share in his glory. I consider that our present sufferings are not worth comparing with the glory that will be revealed in us." The glory far outweighs the suffering, but we must accept the suffering in order to gain the glory.

Chapter 22
In Various Ways

In this book we have looked at over twenty different encounters with God. There does not seem to be a pattern in them. There are no two burning bushes. There are no two men with drawn swords. No two people have the same vision. No two people have the same encounter with God. That is not the way that God works. He works differently with different people. The author of Hebrews put it this way, "In the past God spoke to our forefathers through the prophets at many times and in various ways." (Hebrews 1:1).

There is one similarity in the encounters. God always appears as an adult male if he appears in a human form. He never appears as a female or an animal. This is significant. The people of God were surrounded by female deities, yet God never manifested himself in a female form once. Some may see this as cultural, but since the Israelites from the time they were in bondage in Egypt through their time in Palestine they were surrounded by a host of female deities so the concept of a female deity was certainly not foreign to them. Sometimes they succumbed to the temptation to worship these deities. However, Genesis 1:27 does say, "So God created man in his own image, in the image of God he created him; male and female he created them." There are also a few places in the Bible where God is said to nurture his people. However, all of the names of God in the Bible are masculine. Jesus said in John 4:24, "God is spirit." Can a spiritual being be male or female? Why did God always refer to himself as male in the Bible? Since God is beyond our comprehension, we cannot really answer that question adequately.

There is a progression in the encounters. The more people get to know God, the more reverence they have for him. The further we get into the Bible, the greater the sense of awe people experienced when they encountered God. Actually, this awe and reverence often turned into a sense of fear and dread when the individual realized that he was a sinful creature confronted by the holy Creator.

Jacob is surprised that he survives his encounter with God (Genesis 32:30). Isaiah feared for his life when he had a vision of God in his temple (Isaiah 6:5). Even John, the disciple whom Jesus loved, fell on his face as though dead when he received a vision of the risen Christ (Revelation 1:17). Therefore, if you hear of someone who claims to have had a vision of Christ or God and that vision left him or her with just a warm fuzzy feeling, then you can probably question the legitimacy of that vision. A true encounter with God should inspire awe and reverence if not fear and dread, at least at first. God does calm our fears and bring peace, but first he must reign in our hearts and minds. God must first be our Creator, our King, our Saviour and our Lord before he can be our friend.

I remember one person who thought that the only way that he could truly meet with God was at the altar on Sunday evening. That was the expectation in his church. Now few churches have Sunday evening services. Some people think that you must have a crisis emotional experience similar to theirs or you are not really "born again" and, therefore, not a Christian. Others say that you must have a second experience after conversion in which you speak in tongues. They refer to this experience as the baptism of the Holy Spirit.

The other day I was at a restaurant having dinner with my wife, her niece and her niece's boyfriend. One of my nephews walked into the restaurant with his daughter. My wife started to introduce him to her niece and hesitated a bit with his name. Her problem was not her memory, but the fact that he is an identical twin. She did get his name right. He is over forty and it is much easier to tell him apart from his brother now than it was when they were younger. When they were in school, their teachers often confused them. However, now they are married to and have children. Even today people often tell them apart based on the wife and children that they are with.

We are all different. Every person on the face of this Earth is a unique individual. Even identical twins are different from one another. That is one reason why God treats each of us differently. To expect each of us to have the same experience with God is ridiculous. God made us all different for a reason. He does not want us all to be the same and he does not want to treat us all the same.

This is the main lesson of the book. God is a God of variety. How many different species of plants and animals are there? How many different kinds of people are there? How many different kinds of stars and planets are there in the sky? I could be more specific and talk about the different kinds of insects or birds or reptiles. It was not that long ago that I was at the museum with my grandchildren and I was amazed at the hundreds of different kinds of butterflies on display there. As far as I know, scientists are discovering new species of plants and animals almost daily. Does that not speak to you of a God that loves variety?

When you are dealing with God, expect the unexpected. God may speak in a still small voice or a blinding flash of light or something else entirely. Also, remember the lesson of Joshua. Do not ask God to be on your side. He is in charge. He gives the marching orders. Be willing to say with Isaiah, "Here am I, send me." You may feel inadequate because you are too young, like Jeremiah, or washed up, like Moses, but that does not matter. Who you are is not important. God can use anyone in his service because he is God. Remember nothing is too hard for the LORD.

Also, never lose your sense of wonder. Fall on your knees before the God who created all of those billions of stars. Worship that baby of Bethlehem who Simeon saw as the Saviour of the world through his eyes of faith. Be amazed how Mary could carry the One who created the universe in her womb. Our God is truly worthy of worship no matter how you encounter him.